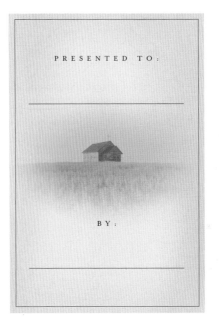

PRESENTED TO:

_____

BY:

_____

Truth

FOR TODAY

A Daily Touch of God's Grace

JOHN
MacArthur

J. COUNTRYMAN
NASHVILLE, TENNESSEE

Project editor: Jenny Baumgartner

Designed by Uttley/DouPonce DesignWorks,
Sisters, Oregon

ISBN 0-8499-9563-9

Printed and bound in Belgium

www.thomasnelson.com

This little book is eagerly dedicated

to all of you who will reach daily

for God's truth and be touched

by His grace every time you do.

Preface

I'll never forget a man I once met while hiking through the mountains of northern California. He was a graduate of Boston University who lived in an overturned Frigidare box by a stream. After I introduced myself to him, he described his frustrating search for the meaning of life.

"Well, have you found the answers?" I asked.

"No," he replied, "but I've put myself into a situation where I don't ask the questions."

Unfortunately, that's the best human wisdom can do.

The last century produced an information explosion unparalleled in human history. Yet modern knowledge has been unable to shed any new light on the most basic spiritual questions facing the human race. That's exactly how the Bible describes mankind in the end times: "always learning and never able to come to the knowledge of the truth" (2 Tim. 3:7).

Man has solved incredibly difficult problems in the fields of mathematics, astronomy, microbiology, and even space travel. But the true meaning of life stubbornly eludes those whose methods of pursuit are purely rational. They end up totally puzzled about life, death, God, man, sin, heaven, hell, love, joy, and peace.

The problem is that spiritual answers cannot be deduced by human reason alone (1 Cor. 2:14). It's not that spiritual truth is irrational or illogical, but that human wisdom is defective, because it's tainted by man's sinfulness, and unable to perceive the things of God.

That is why the Bible is so important. It gives us the answers we can't find on our own. It is God's Word to mankind. Scripture is divinely revealed truth that fills the vacuum of spiritual ignorance in all of us.

So in the year ahead, I hope you'll take a daily dip into the pool of God's truth, and that you'll be touched by His grace every time you do.

JOHN MACARTHUR

Salvation

January

THE POWER OF THE GOSPEL

For I am not ashamed of the gospel of Christ,
for it is the power of God to salvation.

ROMANS 1:16

People want to change. All advertising is based on the presupposition that people want things different from the way they are. They want to look better, feel better, think better, and live better. They want to change their lives but, except from an external standpoint, they are unable to do so.

Only the gospel of Jesus Christ has the power to change people and deliver them from sin, from Satan, from judgment, from death, and from hell. Acts 4:12 says, "Nor is there salvation in any other, for there is no other name under heaven given among men by which we must be saved." And that name is Jesus Christ.

So God's Word, which is all about Jesus Christ, can do for us what we cannot do for ourselves. We are sinful and unable to remedy our condition, but from God comes the incredible, limitless power that can transform our lives.

A SLAVE FOR CHRIST

Let a man so consider us, as servants of Christ.

1 CORINTHIANS 4:1

 The apostle Paul was a "servant" of Christ. It was a role he chose out of love, not fear.

There were perhaps millions of slaves in the Roman Empire. For the most part, they were treated not as persons but as objects. If a master wanted to kill a slave, he could do so without fear of punishment. Though it was a negative term to the Romans, the word *slave* meant dignity, honor, and respect to the Hebrews, and the Greeks considered it a term of humility. As a servant of Christ, then, Paul paradoxically finds himself both exalted and debased. This is the ambivalence every representative of Jesus Christ must face.

When I think of the honor I've been given to preach the gospel of Jesus Christ, I am sometimes overwhelmed. There is no higher calling in life than to proclaim the gospel from the pulpit and to be able to teach the Word of God under the power of the Holy Spirit. Yet there is also a paradox that requires a minister of Christ to realize he does not deserve to minister. He must have the proper perspective of being an unworthy slave who has the incomprehensible privilege of proclaiming the gospel.

NO MORE BAD NEWS

Separated to the gospel of God.

ROMANS 1:1

Thousands of babies are born every day into a world filled with bad news. The term *bad news* has become a colloquialism to describe our era.

Why is there so much bad news? It's simple. The bad news that occurs on a larger scale is only the multiplication of what is occurring on an individual level. The power that makes for bad news is sin.

With so much bad news, can there really be any good news? Yes! The good news is that sin can be dealt with. You don't have to be selfish. Guilt and anxiety can be alleviated. There is meaning to life and hope of life after death. The apostle Paul says in Romans 1:1 that the good news is the gospel. It is the good news that man's sin can be forgiven, guilt can be removed, life can have meaning, and a hopeful future can be a reality.

SEPARATION

It is written, "Be holy, for I am holy."

1 PETER 1:16

Do you know you cannot serve God unless you are *separated*? In the Scripture, that word refers to being set apart for a specific task or purpose.

The Lord said to Moses, "You shall offer up a cake of the first of your ground meal as a heave offering" (Num. 15:20). God wanted the firstfruits of the land to be set apart to honor Him.

The Lord also said, "I the Lord am holy, and have separated you from the peoples, that you should be mine" (Lev. 20:26). God took the nation of Israel and separated them from all other nations for His glory.

In each of these passages in the Septuagint (the Greek version of the Old Testament), the word refers to separation in the fullest sense. The apostle Paul knew that once he was called as an apostle, he would be disconnected from his past. When Paul was the most ardent of Pharisee, he was set apart for—or separated to—the traditions of the Jewish people (Phil. 3:5). Now he could claim to be a Pharisee separated to the gospel of God.

Are you separate from your former life?

Mankind's Box

For in Him dwells all the fullness of the Godhead bodily.

Colossians 2:9

If we were to think of this world as a time-space dimension, then a closed box could represent it, with God outside of the box. It is impossible for mankind to escape the box because, by definition, the natural cannot enter into the supernatural. That which is confined to time and space cannot escape into eternity and infinity.

Because there is something within man that longs to know what is outside the box, he invents deities into existence, which is how religions proliferate. Different religions become an extension of man's desire to escape his box, but man's longing to transcend the box cannot be overcome because he is confined to the box by his very nature.

Is there a way to escape this box? Yes, the good news is there is a way, and it's through Christ. Christianity acknowledges that you can't get out of your box but proclaims that God has invaded the box from the outside. Jesus Christ has entered into your world to show you how you can dwell with God forever. Won't you accept His invitation?

THE INCOMPARABLE CHRIST

He is before all things, and in Him all things consist.

COLOSSIANS 1:17

 Jesus Christ is the most incomparable personality of all human history.

Socrates taught forty years, Plato fifty, and Aristotle forty. Jesus' public ministry lasted less than three years, yet the influence of His life far outweighs the combined 130 years of the three greatest philosophers of all antiquity.

Jesus never painted a picture, yet some of the finest paintings of Raphael, Michelangelo, Da Vinci, and many other artists found in Him their inspiration.

Jesus did not write poetry, but Dante, Milton, and scores of the world's greatest poets have been inspired by Him like no other. Ralph Waldo Emerson said that the name of Jesus "is not so much written as ploughed into the history of this world."

Jesus wrote no music, yet Haydn, Handel, Beethoven, Bach, Mendelssohn, and a myriad of others reached the highest perfection of melody in compositions about Him.

Jesus has affected human society like no other. The incomparable Christ is the good news. And what makes it such good news is that man is so undeserving but that God is so gracious.

A FEW WORDS

Holy men of God spoke as
they were moved by the Holy Spirit.

2 PETER 1:21

Only 297 words are required to sum up in English all of God's moral law in the Ten Commandments. God distilled it even more when He said, "'You shall love the Lord your God with all your heart, with all your soul, and with all your mind.' This is the first and great commandment. And the second is like it, 'You shall love your neighbor as yourself'" (Matt. 22:37–39). Only sixty-five words make up the definitive teaching on prayer—the Lord's Prayer—in Matthew 6:9–13.

Man doesn't have that capacity for essential brevity. There once was a governmental study to regulate the price of cabbage that ran over twenty-six thousand words!

Thank God for the provision of His profound Word.

FULFILLING THE LAW

Therefore you shall be perfect,
just as your Father in heaven is perfect.

MATTHEW 5:48

 Jesus faced much opposition during His ministry when He didn't agree with contemporary Jewish theology (Matt. 15:1–3). Because it was hypocritical, He denied the Pharisees' so-called devotion.

Many in His day were saying, "Is Jesus saying new truth? Is He really speaking for God? He doesn't say what the Pharisees say. He, in fact, says the opposite of what we're taught."

Jesus said, "Do not think that I came to destroy the Law or the Prophets. I did not come to destroy but to fulfill" (Matt. 5:17). Jesus did not condemn Old Testament law, but He did condemn the tradition that had been built up around it. The religious leaders had so perverted God's law that Jesus declared, "I say to you, that unless your righteousness exceeds the righteousness of the scribes and Pharisees, you will by no means enter the kingdom of heaven" (v. 20).

Whose righteousness are you depending on? Your own or Christ's?

Our Consistent Gospel

He promised [the gospel] before
through His Prophets in the Holy Scriptures.

Romans 1:2

Did you know that the Old Testament is completely consistent with the New? That's because the good news is old, not new. The Old Testament, from Genesis to Malachi, or anywhere in between, is all about the revelation of Jesus Christ.

Jesus said that the Scriptures give testimony about Him (John 6:39). In speaking to men on the road to Emmaus, Jesus said, " 'O foolish ones, and slow of heart to believe in all that the prophets have spoken! Ought not the Christ to have suffered these things and to enter into his glory?' And beginning at Moses and all the Prophets, He expounded to them in all the Scriptures the things concerning Himself" (Luke 24:25–27).

Why is that important for you today? So you can be confident that the Scripture holds God's promise of good news in Christ.

THE HISTORICAL JESUS

God has sent His only begotten Son into the world,
that we might live through Him.

1 JOHN 4:9

 Many people doubt whether Jesus ever really existed, but many historians have written about the Lord Jesus Christ.

Around A.D. 114, the Roman historian, Tacitus, wrote that the founder of the Christian religion, Jesus Christ, was put to death by Pontius Pilate in the reign of the Roman Emperor Tiberius (*Annals* 15.44).

Pliny the Younger wrote a letter to the Emperor Trajan on the subject of Christ and Christians (*Letters* 10.96–97).

In A.D. 90, the Jewish historian Josephus penned a short biographical note on Jesus: "Now there was about this time Jesus, a wise man, if it be lawful to call Him a man, for He was a doer of wonderful works, a teacher of such men as received the truth with pleasure. He drew over to Him both many of the Jews and many of the Gentiles. He was Christ" (*Antiquities* 18.63).

The Talmud refers to Jesus of Nazareth (*Sanhedrin* 43a, *Abodah Zerah* 16b–17a).

Jesus was a man in history. And His claims were true. Do you still doubt His ability to save you?

THE AFFIRMATION OF GOD'S SON

Declared to be the Son of God
with power according to the Spirit of holiness,
by the resurrection from the dead.

ROMANS 1:4

Jesus Christ had to be more than a man; He also had to be God. If Jesus were only a man, even the best of men, He could not have saved believers from their sin. If He were even the right man from the seed of David, but not God, He could not have withstood the punishment of God the Father at the cross and risen from the dead. He could not have overcome Satan and the world but would have been conquered as all men are conquered.

If there was ever any question that Jesus was the Son of God, His resurrection from the dead should end it. He had to be man to reach us, but He had to be God to lift us up. When God raised Christ from the dead, He affirmed that what He said was true.

As clearly as the horizon divides the earth from the sky, so the resurrection divides Jesus from the rest of humanity. Jesus Christ is God in human flesh.

A TREASURE STORE

Blessed be the God and Father of our
Lord Jesus Christ, who has blessed us with every
spiritual blessing in the heavenly places in Christ.

EPHESIANS 1:3

There is no way to comprehend the riches God has provided for those who love His Son. The treasures He has prepared are infinite. Jesus said, "The kingdom of heaven is like treasure hidden in a field, which a man found and hid; and for joy over it goes and sells all that he has, and buys that field" (Matt. 13:44). The apostle Paul quotes the prophet Isaiah when he says, "Eye has not seen, nor ear heard, nor have entered into the heart of man the things which God has prepared for those who love him" (1 Cor. 2:9).

The good news is, if we love the Son of God, we inherit all the riches of the Father. If we believe in Christ, we have treasure beyond imagination.

RAISED THROUGH THE SPIRIT

God does not give the Spirit by measure.
The Father loves the Son, and has given
all things into His hand.

JOHN 3:34-35

Jesus took on a role requiring voluntary submission, and He did the will of the Father through the power of the Spirit. That is an amazing act of love and humility from One who is fully God and always will be throughout eternity.

It is important to recognize the Spirit's work in the ministry and resurrection of Jesus because it indicates that the entire Trinity was involved in the redemption of mankind. The greatest affirmation that Jesus is who He claimed to be is that the Father raised the Son through the agency of the Holy Spirit.

A MYSTERIOUS UNION

Taking the form of a bondservant,
and coming in the likeness of men.

PHILIPPIANS 2:7

The humanity and deity of Christ is a mysterious union we can never fully understand. But the Bible emphasizes both.

Luke 23:39–43 provides a good example. At the cross, ". . . one of the criminals who were hanged blasphemed Him, saying, 'If You are the Christ, save Yourself and us.' But the other, answering, rebuked him, saying, 'Do you not even fear God, seeing you are under the same condemnation? And we indeed justly, for we receive the due reward of our deeds; but this Man has done nothing wrong.' Then he said to Jesus, 'Lord, remember me when you come into Your Kingdom.' And Jesus said to him, 'Assuredly, I say to you, today you will be with me in Paradise.'"

In His humanness, Jesus was a victim, mercilessly hammered to a cross after being spat upon, mocked, and humiliated. But in His deity, He promised the thief on the cross eternal life, as only God can.

GRACE FROM THE KING

Being justified freely by His grace through
the redemption that is in Christ Jesus.

ROMANS 3:24

Every believer receives the grace of God as a result of responding to the good news. And the good news is that salvation is by grace.

The apostle Paul said, "For by grace you have been saved through faith, and that not of yourselves; it is the gift of God, not of works, lest anyone should boast" (Eph. 2:8–9). The grace of God that brings salvation has appeared to all people. It is offered totally apart from anything we could ever do to receive God's favor. It is the unmerited favor of God, who in His mercy and loving-kindness grants us salvation as a gift. All we have to do is simply respond by believing in His Son.

We enter the kingdom of God only by the grace of God. There is no place for self-congratulations or human achievement. Remember to thank God for granting you such a gracious salvation.

UNDESERVED FAVOR

Where sin abounded, grace abounded much more.

ROMANS 5:20

Salvation does not come by confirmation, communion, baptism, church membership, church attendance, trying to keep the Ten Commandments, or living out the Sermon on the Mount. It does not come by giving to charity or even by believing that there is a God. It does not come by simply being moral and respectable. Salvation does not even come by claiming to be a Christian. Salvation comes only when we receive by faith the gift of God's grace. Hell will be full of people who tried to reach heaven some other way.

The apostle Paul said, "The law entered that the offense might abound. But where sin abounded, grace abounded much more, so that as sin reigned in death, even so grace might reign through righteousness to eternal life through Jesus Christ our Lord" (Rom. 5:20–21). The first provision of the gospel is grace, which is neither earned nor deserved.

Dr. Donald Grey Barnhouse said, "Love that gives upward is worship; love that goes outward is affection; love that stoops is grace." God has stooped to give us grace. Will you receive it?

Get in the Game

Run in such a way that you might win.

1 Corinthians 9:24

Because I was athletic as a boy, I played on many different teams in various sports programs. I remember many boys with little or no athletic ability who would try out for these teams. Every once in a while, a coach would feel sorry for such a boy and place him on the team in spite of his performance. He would give the boy a uniform to make him feel that he was a part of the team even though he would never let the boy play in a game.

Fortunately, the opposite is true in the Christian life. The Lord doesn't place us on the team just so we can sit on the bench. He intends to send us into the game. It is His grace that calls us to salvation, and it is His will that sends us into the world to witness for Him.

We are all like the boy who had no ability. God graciously puts us on the team, not because of our own ability, but purely by His sovereign grace. And He gives us the ability to play the game. So get in the game and give thanks for the holy privilege of serving Jesus Christ.

COMPELLED TO SERVE

Walk worthy of the calling
with which you were called.

EPHESIANS 4:1

 Do you have any idea of what a high calling it is to serve Christ?

Paul said, "We are His workmanship, created in Christ Jesus for good works, which God prepared beforehand that we should walk in them" (Eph. 2:10). He also said, "I, therefore, the prisoner of the Lord, beseech you to walk worthy of the calling with which you were called" (Eph. 4:1).

In ancient times, a victor at the Olympic Games once asked, "Spartan, what will you gain by this victory?" He replied, "I, sir, shall have the honor to fight on the front line for my king." May that be your response to the call of your King.

JANUARY 19

KNOWN BY OBEDIENCE

*According to the commandment
of the everlasting God, for obedience to the faith.*

ROMANS 16:26

Did you know it's not faith plus obedience that equals salvation, but obedient faith that equals salvation? True faith is verified in your obedience to God.

Because Jesus is Lord, He demands obedience. There is no faith without obedience. Paul said to the Roman Christians, "I thank my God through Jesus Christ for you all, that your faith is spoken of throughout the whole world" (Rom. 1:8). And why was their faith spoken of throughout the world? Romans 16:19 explains: "Your obedience has become known to all." In the beginning, it is your faith that is spread abroad, but in the end it is your obedience.

Faith that excludes obedience won't save anyone. The delusion that it will causes many people to take the broad road that leads to destruction (Matt. 7:13–14). That's like building a religious super-structure on sand (Matt. 7:21–29).

Build your life in obedience to Christ. Then you'll know that you belong to Him.

WHY GOD SAVES

*That grace, having spread through the many,
may cause thanksgiving to abound to the glory of God.*

2 CORINTHIANS 4:15

Many people think the main reason God saves people is so that He can keep them out of hell, or so that they can experience His love or lead happy lives. But all those reasons are secondary.

God saves people because it is an affront to His holy name that someone should live in rebellion against Him. That people experience salvation is not the main issue with God—it is His glory that is at stake.

The apostle Paul said of Jesus, "God also has highly exalted Him and given Him the name which is above every name, that at the name of Jesus every knee should bow, of those in heaven, and of those on earth, and of those under the earth, and that every tongue should confess that Jesus Christ is Lord, to the glory of God the Father" (Phil. 2:9–11). Salvation is for God's glory.

God is glorified when people believe His gospel, love His Son, and accept His diagnosis of their greatest need, which is forgiveness of sin. You certainly benefit from God's provision of salvation, but you exist for the glory of God.

WHOLEHEARTED COMMITMENT

God is my witness, whom I serve with my Spirit.

ROMANS 1:9

Nowadays, we use the word *spirit* in the same way the apostle Paul used it in today's verse. We may watch an athlete go all out in his performance and then comment that he exhibited "spirited" play, which means that his whole being was involved in his effort. When I was in college, the "Esprit de Corps" award was given to the football player who gave the most effort on the field. That is the way in which Paul served the Lord.

Paul never served the Lord without a wholehearted commitment. In so doing, he distinguished himself from the hirelings whose labor was external and insincere (John 10:11–13). So be like Paul—give a wholehearted effort in your service to Christ.

SERVICE AS WORSHIP

Present your bodies a living sacrifice,
holy, acceptable to God, which is
your reasonable service.

ROMANS 12:1

 When many people think of worship, they envision stained-glass windows and pipe organs. But in the Bible, the same word that is used to describe worship also means service.

The greatest worship you ever render to God is to serve Him. For Paul, service meant a total commitment.

Paul wrote to Timothy, "I thank God, whom I serve with a pure conscience" (2 Tim. 1:3). Paul was saying that you could look deep inside him and see that he served God with his entire being. Paul's service was an act of worship. It was deep, genuine, and honest. That is the real measure of true spirituality. The only way to serve God is with total commitment.

TRUE THANKS

*I thank my God through Jesus Christ
for you all, that your faith is spoken of
throughout the whole world.*

ROMANS 1:8

One thing we know about the apostle Paul: he had a thankful heart. In almost every one of his epistles, Paul expressed thanks for the people who would receive his message. Though he knew that each church needed correction, he didn't just send instruction; he also sent a word of thanks. He was always able to see God's purposes being accomplished. Paul expressed what is in the heart of all true servants of God—an attitude of gratitude.

Unfortunately, some people go through life dwelling on the negative. They refuse to be grateful for the good that God is doing in someone else's life. If it isn't happening to them, then they think it's bad. Paul didn't express his thanks by saying, "I'm so thankful for what God has done for *me*"; rather, he said, "I thank God for *you*." He received as much joy from someone else's success as he did from his own. May the same be true of you as well.

A Thankful Heart

I thank my God upon every remembrance of you.

PHILIPPIANS 1:3

 A thankful heart is essential for true spiritual service. If you are trying to serve the Lord without gratitude in your heart for what He's done for you, then you are serving in the flesh with improper motives. One who is thankful realizes that God has a cause for everything that happens. One who serves externally, legalistically, or ritualistically will not find very many things to be thankful for in his life because he is not grateful for the things God has already done for him.

Do you have a thankful heart? Are you overwhelmed with thanksgiving for what God has done? If you are, then you will be free from bitterness or resentment toward God or anyone else.

There is so much to be thankful for. The devil often tempts us by saying, "You deserve better than that. You don't have to be thankful." But when he does, make sure you remember how much you have to be thankful for!

It Doesn't Seem Right

For if I preach the gospel, I have nothing to boast of,
for necessity is laid upon me; yes, woe is me if I preach not
the gospel! For if I do this willingly, I have a reward.

1 Corinthians 9:16–17

There is a story of an old missionary who was returning home from Africa. He was on the same ship with President Teddy Roosevelt who had been in Africa for a big game hunt. When the ship docked in New York, great crowds greeted the president, but the old missionary and his wife walked off the ship unnoticed.

"It just doesn't seem right," said the missionary to his wife in a rather bitter tone. "We give our lives in Africa to win souls to Christ, and when we arrive home, there's no reward or anyone to meet us. The president shoots some animals and gets a royal welcome." As they were praying before they went to bed, the missionary sensed that the Lord was saying to him, "Do you know why you haven't received your reward yet? Because you're not home."

That's what Paul had in mind in his spiritual service. He didn't want to receive superficial or temporal acclaim. He was willing to wait until he went home—his ultimate home—to receive what God had promised him. Are you willing to wait?

IS ANYONE LISTENING?

I will very gladly spend and be spent
for your souls; though the more abundantly
I love you, the less I am loved.

2 CORINTHIANS 12:15

There have been times in my ministry as a pastor that I've wondered if anyone is listening to what I'm teaching. Do people really appreciate me or the teaching of the Word? It's easy to fall into that kind of woe-is-me complex.

Maybe you've felt the same way in your ministry. If so, you must remember that as long as you look at the ministry you're in as something you *give*, you will never have that problem. But if you look at the ministry as something you *get*, you will end up with a twisted view of what real ministry is.

If you're ever tempted to view your ministry with a selfish attitude, adopt the attitude Paul exhibited in today's verse. Even if the people hated him, he would still love them. The main characteristic of love is unselfish giving.

SOMETHING OF ETERNAL VALUE

I long to see you, that I may impart to you
some spiritual gift, so that you may be established.

ROMANS 1:11

Some years ago, a young woman in our church who was a student at a local university said to me, "I learned a great lesson from one of your sermons on love. I always told myself that I loved the little girls in my fourth-grade Sunday school class. They all have small, frilly dresses and the cutest smiles."

She went on to say, "One Saturday I was attending a football game at my school—something I do every Saturday—and the Lord convicted me about not adequately preparing my Sunday school lesson. Because I attended the games on Saturday, I was in the habit of teaching a lesson on Sunday morning that was very shallow and superficial. God pointed out that I didn't really love those girls the way I thought I did because I made no sacrifice in my own life to give them something of eternal value."

She ended our conversation by saying, "So from now on, I will not be attending any more football games until my lesson is completed and I feel I can impart to them something of eternal value."

GIVE YOURSELF

*We were well pleased to impart
to you not only the gospel of God,
but also our own lives.*

1 THESSALONIANS 2:8

I had the privilege of attending seminary to study for the ministry. I learned much from the books I read, the notes I took, and the papers I wrote. But I learned far more from the lives of the men who taught me. Rather than focusing on what they said, I concentrated on why they said it.

That is what Paul did with the Romans. He, in effect, said, "Before I give you my theology, let me give you myself." Paul is a model for all who serve Christ. Follow Paul's example and begin giving yourself.

THE PRESSURE OF MINISTRY

*The hardworking farmer
must be first to partake of the fruits.*

2 TIMOTHY 2:6

A person who serves with his whole heart will be content only with spiritual fruit. Yet some will only be content with prestige, acceptance, or money.

In the past, Satan has tried to put that thought into my mind. At times he's tried to make me question why I care about the people I minister to. His approach is to make me secure in the knowledge that I'm saved and going to heaven, that I'm well paid in a good job with a lot of security. But that is Satan's lie.

It's very easy to let Satan pressure you into settling for less than God's best. When Satan plants thoughts like that in my head, my reaction is: I am not content to simply be taken care of or appreciated. What matters is bearing fruit. Make the focus of your ministry spiritual fruit.

AN OBLIGATION TO GOD

*I am debtor both to the Greeks and
to the barbarians; both to the wise
and to the unwise.*

ROMANS 1:14

A young man once asked me what motivates me to study week after week. I told him that sometimes, the Scripture passages are so exhilarating that I can't wait to get to Sunday to preach. But then there are other times when I battle against priorities that crowd out my study time, and my ministry doesn't seem that exciting then. I really have to fight my way through those times because I know I have a debt to God.

What if I see a house on fire, and the family inside is unaware of their dire situation? I cannot stand on the curb and wonder if they're worth saving. Because they are in need and I have the information that can save them, I have an obligation to them.

If you are involved in Christian service only when you feel like doing it, you haven't learned the kind of service Paul described in today's verse. When facing a tough period in ministering to people, sometimes all you can rely on is your obligation to God.

EAGER FOR SERVICE

So, as much as is in me,
I am ready to preach the gospel to
you who are in Rome also.

ROMANS 1:15

Are you happy and eager to fulfill the responsibility God has committed to your care? As you can tell from today's verse, that was Paul's attitude. He was consumed with doing the work of the ministry. His personal life was never the issue. Life had only one purpose for him, and that was doing the will of God. He was always eager to preach.

Paul was like a racehorse in the gate or a sprinter in the blocks—waiting to gain the victory. God had to hold him back once in a while because he was so ready to go. Are you as eager? Is that the kind of service you render, or does someone have to prod you along with all their might just to get you involved? If your service to Christ comes from your whole heart, then you will be eager.

Foundations

FEBRUARY

THE KEY TO
SPIRITUAL GROWTH

Grow in the grace and knowledge
of our Lord and Savior Jesus Christ.
To Him be the glory both now and forever. Amen.

2 PETER 3:18

Spiritual growth is not mystical, sentimental, devotional, or psychological. It's not the result of some clever secret or formula. It is simply matching your practice with your position.

As believers, our position in Christ is perfect: we are complete in Him (Col. 2:10); we have all things that pertain to life and godliness (2 Pet. 1:3); and we have received all spiritual blessings (Eph. 1:3). But now we need to progress in our daily lives in a way that is commensurate with our exalted position.

Today's verse provides the most important concept in understanding and experiencing spiritual growth. Giving glory to God is directly related to spiritual growth. Therefore, it is vital that we understand what it means to glorify Him.

FOCUSING ON GOD'S GLORY

I have set the Lord always before me.

PSALM 16:8

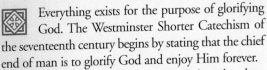 Everything exists for the purpose of glorifying God. The Westminster Shorter Catechism of the seventeenth century begins by stating that the chief end of man is to glorify God and enjoy Him forever.

Psalm 19:1 says, "The heavens declare the glory of God." The vastness of space and all therein glorifies God.

In Isaiah 43:20, God says, "The beast of the field will honor Me."

The angels who appeared at the birth of Christ said, "Glory to God in the highest" (Luke 2:14).

Scripture explains that you exist to give God glory. May you follow the lead of David and set the Lord always before you.

RESPONDING TO GOD'S GLORY

We all, with unveiled face, beholding as in a mirror
the glory of the Lord, are being transformed into the same
image from glory to glory, just as by the Spirit of the Lord.
2 CORINTHIANS 3:18

As we glorify God, we begin to grow. Because of the great truths revealed in the New Testament, believers can now view God's glory more clearly than those under the law could. As we do, we grow spiritually, moving from one level of glory to the next.

At the end of today's verse, notice that Paul says the Holy Spirit is the one who energizes our growth. The Holy Spirit infuses our lives with His power, taking us through levels of glory toward the image of Christ.

Don't become preoccupied with the intricacies of the Holy Spirit's work or with the details of your own activity. Make sure you focus primarily on the glory of the Lord.

SPIRITUAL PROGRESSION

*I write to you, fathers, because you have known Him
who is from the beginning. I write to you, young men,
because you have overcome the wicked one. I write to you,
little children, because you have known the Father.*

1 JOHN 2:13

My own experience has taught me much about the different levels of spiritual growth described by the apostle John in today's verse. When I was a spiritual babe, I was lost in the euphoria of loving the Lord and didn't know much theology. At that time I was easily influenced by anyone's teaching. Later, as I learned the Word of God, false doctrine no longer deceived me; it made me angry. And now, as I have grown in my knowledge of the Word, it's my desire to know God more intimately, which is the final level of growth. Spiritual fathers not only know the Bible, but also know deeply the God who wrote it.

Spiritual growth progresses from knowing you are a Christian to knowing the Word of God to knowing God Himself. The way to know God is to spend your life focusing on His glory, thus learning to understand the fullness of His person. That focus becomes a magnet drawing you upward through the levels of maturity.

WHY WE WITNESS

By this My Father is glorified,
that you bear much fruit;
so you will be My disciples.

JOHN 15:8

Most people probably think we should be saved for reasons other than to glorify God. Many Christians will usually give the following as the reasons they witness:

- To keep people out of hell. They want them to avoid eternal punishment.
- To manifest God's love.
- To obey Christ's command. In Matthew 28:18–20 and Acts 1:8, Jesus tells us to evangelize.

Those are all valid, biblical reasons for evangelism, but the main reason we should preach the gospel is for the glory of God.

CONFESSING JESUS AS LORD

*If you confess with your mouth the Lord Jesus
and believe in your heart that God has raised
Him from the dead, you will be saved.*

ROMANS 10:9

To give glory to Christ, we must confess Him as Lord. That's a part of salvation, not a subsequent act. Salvation is a matter of confessing that Christ is God and, therefore, that He is sovereign in your life.

If you have never confessed Jesus Christ as Lord, you have no capacity to live for His glory. You cannot say, "I deny Christ. He is not my Savior or Lord," and then expect to glorify God. If you dishonor the Son, you dishonor the Father (John 5:23). So salvation is the necessary beginning for glorifying God and, therefore, for spiritual growth. You cannot grow until you are born.

THE AIM OF YOUR LIFE

Whether you eat or drink,
or whatever you do, do all to the glory of God.

1 CORINTHIANS 10:31

When you confessed Jesus as Lord, you did so to the glory of God. Now whatever else you do—even the most mundane functions of life such as eating and drinking—should be focused on the glory of God. That should be the underlying attitude of your life.

Jesus observed His focus in this way: "I honor My Father. . . . I do not seek My own glory" (John 8:49, 50). You will grow spiritually when you follow Christ's example of submitting your life to Christ's lordship, you will be characterized by His humble desire to glorify the Father.

CONSUMED WITH GOD'S GLORY

You cannot bear those who are evil.

We should be so consumed with God's glory that we hurt when He is dishonored. That was certainly the attitude of David when he said, "Because zeal for Your house has eaten me up, and the reproaches of those who reproach You have fallen on me" (Ps. 69:9). David was deeply hurt when God was dishonored.

As a father, I understand what David was saying. If you hurt someone in my family, you hurt me. Often I have cried for someone I love whose heart was broken. When you identify with God in that way, you will care about His honor much more than about what happens to you.

Feeling What God Feels

Whether we live or die, we are the Lord's.

Romans 14:8

I remember one young woman who learned to feel pain when God was dishonored. She left a little town in West Virginia to live with a guy who was a student at UCLA. After a while, he kicked her out. She wandered around and tried to take her life several times, but each time she survived. My sister and I met her and had the opportunity to lead her to Christ. Soon after that she decided to go back to her hometown so she could tell her mother and friends about Christ.

Several months later, she wrote me a letter. This is some of what she wrote:

"I can almost feel the unbearable sadness that God feels when someone rejects and doesn't glorify Him. He's God! He made us. He gave us everything. We continue to doubt and reject Him. It's awful! When I think of how I hurt Him, I hope I can someday make it up.

"It's all so clear to me that God must be glorified. He deserves it, and it's long overdue. I can't wait to just tell Jesus, and thus God indirectly, that I love Him. I want God to be God and to take His rightful place. I'm tired of the way people put Him down."

CONFRONTING AN EVIL WORLD

*If you are reproached for the name of Christ,
blessed are you, for the Spirit of glory
and of God rests upon you.*

1 PETER 4:14

No one can live for God's glory and be entirely comfortable in this world. You shouldn't be obnoxious or try to be a misfit, but if your life is Christlike, then you will bear some of the reproach He bore.

We live in a day when many want to make Christianity easy, but the Bible says it is hard. Many want to make Christians lovable, but God says they'll be reproachable. Christianity must confront the system by being distinct from it. It must expose sin before it can disclose the remedy.

Be sure your life reflects your commitment to Christ. That's what will make you distinct from the world.

THE SUCCESS SYNDROME

If I am being poured out
as a drink offering on the sacrifice and service
of your faith, I am glad and rejoice with you all.

PHILIPPIANS 2:17

American society is breeding a generation of Christians who primarily want to be successful. Seldom do they have a humble attitude of service. They are unwilling to make sacrifices for the cause of Christ because they have been taught, whether verbally or not, that Christians should be rich, famous, successful, and popular.

Such an orientation toward personal success rather than humble service is the opposite of what glorifies God. Living for the glory of God means knowing you are expendable and being ready to die, if necessary, to accomplish God's ends. Such a humble attitude glorifies God.

To grow spiritually, we must lose ourselves in the lordship of Christ at the moment of salvation and allow Him to dominate our lives from then on. In doing so, we must seek only His glory—not our own comfort and success. We will not grow when we choose our own way or serve God with the wrong motive.

DROPPING THE DEAD WEIGHT

Let us lay aside every weight, and the
sin which so easily ensnares us, and let us run
with endurance the race that is set before us.

HEBREWS 12:1

Whenever we excuse our sin, we are blaming God. Adam did that when God questioned Him about eating the forbidden fruit. He answered, "The woman whom You gave to be with me, she gave me of the tree, and I ate" (Gen. 3:12). Adam did not accept responsibility for his sin but blamed God, who had given Eve to him.

Sin is never God's fault, nor is it the fault of a person or circumstance that God brings into our lives. Excusing sin impugns God for something that is our fault alone. If He chooses to chasten us, we deserve it.

That's why confession of sin is essential to spiritual growth. When you openly face the reality of your sin and confess it, you have less dead weight to drag you down in the process of growth. As today's verse indicates, your growth will increase as the weight of sin drops off through confession.

TAKE RESPONSIBILITY

Against You, You only, have I sinned,
and done this evil in Your sight.

PSALM 51:4

If you want to have a decreasing frequency of sin in your life and an increasing amount of spiritual growth, you must acknowledge your responsibility. Don't blame your circumstances, your husband, your wife, your boyfriend, your girlfriend, your boss, your employees, or your pastor. Don't even blame the devil. Your sin is your fault. Certainly the world's system can contribute to the problem, but sin ultimately occurs as an act of the will—and you are responsible for it.

Perhaps one of the best examples of someone who learned how to take responsibility was the prodigal son. When he returned home to his loving father, he said, "Father, I have sinned against heaven and in your sight, and am no longer worthy to be called your son" (Luke 15:21). He was even willing to be treated as a humble laborer because he knew he didn't deserve anything (v. 19). That is the right attitude of one who confesses sin.

A Mark of the Christian

If we confess our sins,
He is faithful and just to forgive us our sins.

1 John 1:9

The apostle John wrote his first epistle to define the difference between a Christian and an unbeliever. Our verse for today indicates that confession characterizes the former. The next verse says, "If we say that we have not sinned, we make Him a liar" (v. 10). Unregenerate men deny their sin, but Christians take responsibility for it and confess it.

Confession of sin doesn't take place only at salvation. It continues, as faith does, throughout the life of a believer. A willingness to confess sin is part of the pattern of life that characterizes every believer. That pattern also includes love (1 John 3:14), separation from the world (2:15), and instruction by the Holy Spirit (2:27). Of course there are varying degrees of confession—sometimes we don't make as full a confession as we should—but a true believer eventually acknowledges his sin.

THE NECESSITY OF REPENTANCE

Create in me a clean heart, O God,
and renew a steadfast spirit within me.
PSALM 51:10

True confession cannot happen without repentance. Many times we don't confess our sin because we're not ready to let go of it. When I was a young Christian, I remember telling the Lord that I was sorry about particular sins I had committed and then thanked Him for already forgiving them. But that was all I did.

I reached a milestone in my spiritual life when I began to say, "Lord, thank You for forgiving those sins. I know they did not please You, and I never want to do them again." That can be hard to say because sometimes we want to commit certain sins again. But we betray a lack of spiritual maturity when we want to eliminate the penalty of sin but retain the pleasure. For your confession to be genuine, you must turn from your sins.

OUR DEFENSE MECHANISM

If I regard iniquity in my heart,
the Lord will not hear.

According to today's verse, you cannot even commune with God, let alone grow spiritually, if you are harboring sin. That's why confession is so vital.

You must first be willing to accept God's chastening for your sin. If you think He is being too rough, you should examine your life to see if you deserve it. For the same reason parents must provide consequences for a child's misbehavior, God chastens you so that you don't repeat your mistakes.

God also has placed a system of guilt in you for your own good. Spiritual life without guilt would be like physical life without pain. Guilt is a defense mechanism; it's like an alarm that goes off to lead you to confession when you sin. That's when you need to confront your sin and acknowledge to God that it is an affront to Him. That admission must be a part of your life before you can ever grow spiritually, because it eliminates the sin that holds you back.

DO YOU REALLY BELIEVE GOD?

[Abraham] did not waver at the promise of God through unbelief, but was strengthened in faith, giving glory to God.

ROMANS 4:20

Professing to believe what God has said is much easier than really trusting Him. For instance, many people who affirm that "God shall supply all your need according to His riches" (Phil. 4:19) become filled with anxiety when financial troubles come their way.

The Bible also says that if we give sacrificially with the proper motives, God will reward us (Matt. 6:3–4). Many say they believe that principle as well, but they find it difficult to put into practice. Many Christians also fear death, even though God has said He will provide us with the grace we need to face it and will take us to heaven afterward.

Believing God means we acknowledge His glory, which is the sum of all His attributes and the fullness of all His majesty. If He is who He says He is, then He is to be believed. You will grow spiritually when you say to God, "If Your Word says it, I will believe it; if Your Word promises it, I will claim it; and if Your Word commands it, I will obey it."

GROWING BY FAITH

We walk by faith, not by sight.

2 CORINTHIANS 5:7

Today's verse refers to the walk of becoming more like Christ. It takes place when we live by faith. When we judge everything by what we see, however, we will have difficulty growing.

Remember the twelve spies Israel sent into Canaan (Num. 13)? Ten came back and said they felt like grasshoppers in a land of giants. Those ten walked by sight. But Joshua and Caleb had faith, knowing that God was on their side. Ten didn't think God could handle the circumstances, but two knew He is bigger than any situation.

Do you live by faith? If you want to grow spiritually, believe God's Word and trust Him in every situation.

BEARING FRUIT

He who abides in Me,
and I in Him, bears much fruit.

JOHN 15:5

We had a peach tree in our backyard, and one year it went wild with fruit. We had enough peaches to feed the whole neighborhood! Another year, we could find only one tiny, shriveled peach. Some Christians can be like that, exhibiting little evidence of belonging to God—but God wants us to grow and produce much fruit for His glory.

The fruit you bear is the manifestation of your character, and the only way people will know that you are a child of God. He wants to present Himself to the world through what He produces in you, so His character is at stake in your fruit. He wants you to be fruitful far above what the world or the flesh can produce.

Types of Spiritual Fruit

Walk worthy of the Lord, fully pleasing Him,
being fruitful in every good work.

Colossians 1:10

What kind of fruit brings glory to God? Philippians 1:11 says, "Being filled with the fruits of righteousness which are by Jesus Christ, to the glory and praise of God." Righteousness, which is doing right, is the fruit God desires in our lives. When we do right, we glorify God; when we do wrong, we dishonor Him. Fruit is synonymous with righteousness.

There are two kinds of spiritual fruit: action fruit—which consists of giving, leading others to Christ, and expressing thanks to God—and attitude fruit. Galatians 5:22–23 describes attitude fruit: "The fruit of the Spirit is love, joy, peace, longsuffering, kindness, goodness, faithfulness, gentleness, self-control."

How do you get the right attitudes? Verse 25 says, "If we live in the Spirit, let us also walk in the Spirit." As you yield control of your life to the Holy Spirit, He will permeate your life and produce the proper fruit.

ASPECTS OF PRAISE

Whoever offers praise glorifies Me.

PSALM 50:23

 What does it mean to praise God? According to the Bible, praise involves three things:

1. *Reciting God's attributes.* One great reason to study the Old Testament is that it so powerfully reveals the character of God, enabling us to praise Him better.

2. *Reciting God's works.* The psalms are filled with lists of the great things God has done. He parted the Red Sea, brought His people out of Egypt, made water flow from a rock, fed Israel in the wilderness with manna from heaven, and did many other powerful works. When you praise God for all that He has done, your problems pale in comparison. Remembering God's past performance glorifies Him and strengthens our faith.

3. *Giving thanks for God's attributes and works.* At the heart of praise is thanksgiving. Praising God gives Him glory. No matter what happens in our lives, we are to express our thanks to Him for all His attributes and gracious works.

LOVING OBEDIENCE

He who has My commandments
and keeps them, it is he who loves Me.

JOHN 14:21

If I could simplify the Christian life to one thing, it would be obedience. I don't mean just external obedience but a spirit of obedience. It's not like the little girl who defiantly continued to stand up after her father had told her many times to sit down. Finally her father said, "Sit down, or I'll spank you." She sat down but looked up and said, "I'm sitting down, but I'm standing up in my heart!" That's obeying outwardly but disobeying in the heart. A Christian should be *willing* to obey.

One evidence of spiritual maturity is loving God enough to obey Him even when it is difficult. God is glorified when we willingly obey Him no matter what the cost. Each time we obey, we grow spiritually, and each time we disobey, we retard our growth.

Why God Answers Prayer

Whatever you ask in My name, that I will do,
that the Father may be glorified in the Son.

John 14:13

Why does God answer prayer? The last part of today's verse gives the answer: He answers prayer for His sake as well as ours. He does it to put Himself on display. Understanding this concept increases our confidence in prayer: we can know God will answer because it is an opportunity for Him to receive glory. We will grow spiritually as we interact with God through prayer and see His power on display.

The context of John 14:13 shows that the disciples were greatly distressed because Jesus told them He would be leaving. The disciples had relied on Jesus for so long that they feared being without Him. He had provided all their resources. He was their beloved friend and their spiritual, theological, and economic resource. He was their future as well as their present. They panicked at the thought of His leaving, but He left them and us the promise of John 14:13—whatever we need and ask for in His name, He will do.

A PRAYER PREREQUISITE

If we ask anything according to His will,
He hears us.

1 JOHN 5:14

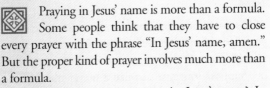 Praying in Jesus' name is more than a formula. Some people think that they have to close every prayer with the phrase "In Jesus' name, amen." But the proper kind of prayer involves much more than a formula.

What does it mean to pray in Jesus' name? In Scripture, the name of God embodies all that He is. When God told Moses His name, He said, "I am who I am" (Ex. 3:14). Likewise, Jesus' name embodies all that He is. When you pray in His name, what you ask should be consistent with who He is. Praying in Jesus' name is praying in accord with God's will.

When our requests are in line with God's sovereign plan, He will answer them and our faith will increase. Instead of invoking a formula at the end of your prayers, perhaps you could say, "I pray this because I believe it to be the will of Christ."

PRAISE FOR ANSWERS

Pray without ceasing, in everything give thanks.

1 THESSALONIANS 5:16–17

When God answers prayers about a particular situation, we have the privilege of being a part of His work and of praising Him for it. When we don't participate through prayer, we miss the opportunity to give Him glory.

Suppose someone came to a prayer meeting and said, "I've had the most wonderful thing happen: the lady I've been witnessing to has opened her heart to Christ. She is now a believer and is here with us tonight. Thank you for praying for her these last few months." The people present can praise the Lord, especially those who had been praying for this woman's conversion.

But there would also be some who, while offering praise, would not have felt a sense of being involved because they had not prayed for the lady. You need to be in on what God is doing so you can offer heartfelt praise.

HANDLING GOD'S WORD

These words which I command you today shall be in your heart.
You shall teach them diligently to your children,
and shall talk of them when you sit in your house,
when you walk by the way, when you lie down,
and when you rise up.

DEUTERONOMY 6:6–7

Spiritual growth cannot occur without the regular intake of God's Word, just as physical growth cannot occur without regular food intake—that's why eating is a daily necessity! Going to church on Sunday to hear a message and then hoping that it is enough to last for the whole week is like eating dinner on Sunday and expecting it to sustain you until the following Sunday. You need to eat every day of the week. The same is true spiritually: there must be a daily feeding on the Word of God for optimum growth.

Mature Christians know that there is even greater glory in giving out the Word than in feeding on it. As you proclaim the Word, you cement it in your life. In this way, the saying "The more you give away, the more you keep" is true. I have found that I tend to remember the things I teach to others but forget the things I read and never pass on. So give a high priority to passing on to others what you're learning from God's Word each day.

APPLYING THE PRINCIPLES

Grow up in all things into Him who is the head—Christ.
Ephesians 4:15

Spiritual growth is simply a matter of applying scriptural principles, but there are many who believe only spiritual giants experience a great increase in faith.

I have read about mystics who knelt and prayed for eight to ten hours, wearing holes in the wood floors. I have read about Robert Murray McCheyne, who would soil the pages of his Bible and the wood of his pulpit with great floods of tears. And I have read *Power Through Prayer* by E. M. Bounds, who spent countless hours in prayer. As I learned about these people, all I could think of was that I could never reach that level. But God uses each of us in different ways.

Spiritual growth is not some mystical achievement for a select few on a higher spiritual plane. Rather, it is simply a matter of glorifying God by confessing sin, trusting Him, bearing fruit, praising Him, obeying and proclaiming His Word, praying, and leading others to Christ. Those are the qualities every Christian needs in order to mature. When you focus on them, the Spirit of God will change you into the image of Christ, from one level of glory to the next.

The Accountability Factor

Let us consider one another
in order to stir up love and good works.

I have found that the closer I am to the godly people around me, the easier it is for me to live a righteous life because they hold me accountable. If something isn't right in my life, they point it out to me. God has given me a wife and four grown children who expect me to walk a righteous path. If I stray from it, one or sometimes all five of them will inform me that I am out of line.

It's easy to begin thinking that if you try your best, you can live a spiritual life without being involved in a church or having close, godly friends. This may be possible, but you'll have a difficult time growing in your faith. Accountability applies a helpful pressure toward godliness. May today's verse guide you toward stronger spiritual patterns.

Discipleship

MARCH

WHO IS A DISCIPLE?

He who does not take his cross
and follow after Me is not worthy of Me.

MATTHEW 10:38

A disciple is someone who confesses Christ as Lord and Savior, believes that God has raised Him from the dead, and declares that belief publicly through baptism. He is not some sort of "upper-level" Christian.

You don't have to wait to become a disciple at some future time in your Christian life when you have reached a certain level of maturity. According to Matthew 28:19–20, a disciple is made at the moment of salvation.

Some claim that there are many Christians who are not disciples. They recall today's verse and say that in order to be a disciple, one has to deny himself, take up his cross, and follow Christ. If one is not up to that level of commitment, they think, then he is not worthy to be Christ's disciple. But you cannot separate discipleship from conversion.

When someone is saved, he receives a submissive spirit that manifests itself by a willingness to make a public confession and obey whatever else Christ commands. Are you, then, a disciple?

A VIEW TO OBEDIENCE

*Teaching them to observe all things
that I have commanded you.*

MATTHEW 28:20

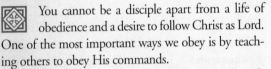 You cannot be a disciple apart from a life of obedience and a desire to follow Christ as Lord. One of the most important ways we obey is by teaching others to obey His commands.

Regarding the Holy Spirit, Jesus said, "He will teach you all things, and bring to your remembrance all things I said to you" (John 14:26). Through the Word of God, the Spirit has made that teaching available to every believer. And every believer is to submit himself to it in obedience.

Only a true convert will obey Christ. Only as you "present yourselves to God as being alive from the dead, and your members as instruments of righteousness to God" (Rom. 6:13) do you exhibit obedient faith.

The End of Growth

Everyone who has
this hope in Him purifies Himself.

1 John 3:3

Second Peter 3:18 commands believers to "grow in the grace and knowledge of our Lord and Savior Jesus Christ." Your response to this verse is either action or inaction. If you desire to mature in Christ, you will experience blessing, usefulness, and victory by following the biblical path of glorifying God. And as David discovered, you will also experience joy: "I have set the Lord always before me. . . . Therefore my heart is glad" (Ps. 16:8, 9).

The apostle John summed up the goal of spiritual growth when he said, "Beloved, now we are children of God; and it has not yet been revealed what we shall be, but we know that when He is revealed, we shall be like Him, for we shall see Him as He is" (1 John 3:2). The growth process will end on the day that we see Jesus Christ and become like Him.

MATURITY IN SUFFERING

May the God of all grace, who called us to His eternal
glory by Christ Jesus, after you have suffered a while,
perfect, establish, strengthen, and settle you.

1 PETER 5:10

A Christian's call to glory necessitates walking the path of suffering. Today's verse explains why. Suffering is God's way of maturing His people spiritually. He is pleased when we patiently endure the suffering that comes our way. Suffering is a part of God's plan to prepare His people for glory.

The apostle Peter said this regarding the value of suffering: "You greatly rejoice, though now for a little while, if need be, you have been grieved by various trials, that the genuineness of your faith, being much more precious than gold that perishes, though it is tested by fire, may be found to praise, honor, and glory at the revelation of Jesus Christ" (1 Pet. 1:6–7). God allows suffering as a validation of our faith. It also produces patience, though patience is a quality we won't need in eternity—there will be no reason for *im*patience there. But beyond those benefits, suffering increases our capacity to praise, honor, and glorify God—and that's something we will use throughout eternity.

READY TO SUFFER

Since Christ suffered for us in the flesh,
arm yourselves also with the same mind.

1 PETER 4:1

One of the blessings of being a Christian is our identification with Christ and its resulting privileges. However, just so we won't take those blessings for granted, assuming that they will result in our being loved and respected by the world, God also allows us to suffer. In fact, the apostle Peter in his first epistle clearly shows that those most blessed in the faith suffer the most.

The Christian life is a call to glory through a journey of suffering. That's because those in Christ are inevitably at odds with their culture and society. All Satan-energized systems are actively at odds with the things of Christ. The apostle John said a person can't love both God and the world (1 John 2:15), and James said, "Whoever therefore wants to be a friend of the world makes himself an enemy of God" (James 4:4).

CALLED TO SUFFER

For to this [suffering] you were called.

1 PETER 2:21

Though today's verse seems to point out that we are called to suffer, it actually refers back to the last part of verse 20, which says, "When you do good and suffer, if you take it patiently, this is commendable before God." When Christians endure suffering with patience, it pleases God.

That shouldn't surprise us. Earlier in this chapter of First Peter, the apostle Peter states that Christians "are a chosen generation, a royal priesthood, a holy nation, His own special people, that you may proclaim the praises of Him who called you out of darkness into His marvelous light" (v. 9). Our dark world resents and is often hostile toward those who represent the Lord Jesus Christ. That resentment and hostility may be felt at certain times and places more than others, but it is always there to some extent as a part of the privilege of being His own.

WHAT DO
YOU REALLY LOVE?

*If anyone comes to Me and does not hate his father and mother,
wife and children, brothers and sisters, yes, and his own life also,
he cannot be My disciple. And whoever does not bear his cross
and come after Me cannot be my disciple.*

LUKE 14:26–27

Apart from God, nothing could have been dearer to Abraham than his son Isaac. But that was the test: to find out whether he loved Isaac more than God. If we love God supremely, we will thank Him for what He is accomplishing through our trials and sufferings. But if we love ourselves more than God, we will question God's wisdom and become upset and bitter. If anything is dearer to us than God, then He must remove it for us to grow spiritually.

In today's verse, Jesus was not indicating that we're to hate everyone. Rather He meant that if you do not love God to the degree that you willingly, if necessary, cut yourself off from your father, mother, spouse, children, brother, sister, or even your own life, then you don't love Him supremely. You must determine to do the will of God first and foremost, no matter what appeals others may make to you.

A LIVING HOPE

*His abundant mercy has
begotten us again to a living hope.*

1 PETER 1:3

When God saved you and transformed you, He gave you "an inheritance incorruptible and undefiled and that does not fade away" (1 Pet. 1:4). As a result, Christians can live in the hope of that eternal inheritance.

Why is this hope important? Unbelievers do not trust Him, so they cannot hope in Him. But as a believer, you have seen that God has been faithful in your past and present and that gives you the hope that He will be faithful in the future. And that gives Him glory.

Simply put, God is glorified when you trust Him. He's glorified when you believe Him. And He is glorified when you hope in His future promise. The God who has given you such a great salvation is worthy of your hope.

The Thrill of Grace

For of His fullness we have all received,
and grace upon grace.

Is the experience of God's grace in your life a thrilling thing? It is for me! Just thinking about the fact that God, by His own sovereign plan, decided to be gracious to me is overwhelming.

He poured out His grace on me. He forgave all my sins. He granted me the indwelling of the Holy Spirit. He gave me an understanding of His Word. He called me to spiritual ministry. Every day He gives me a rich communion with the saints, and I relish being a part of His redeemed people. He enables me to see the world as His handiwork. I am His child, and He loves me in a personal way.

There is nothing greater than receiving grace upon grace. I pray that is your experience.

RIGHT PRIORITIES

Set your mind on things above,
not on things on the earth.

COLOSSIANS 3:2

 Where are your priorities? Are you focused on things of this world, or on spiritual issues? Would the coming of Jesus Christ tomorrow mess up your plans? Unfortunately, many Christians hope He doesn't show up for a while.

What a sad commentary! If you would rather stay on earth than be in Christ's glorious home in heaven, then you don't love His appearing. It grieves God when we don't live in anticipation of His glorious presence and are more interested in the mundane passing things of this world.

Where is your heart? It's time to take a close look at your priorities. When you're truly grateful for the salvation God has given, then you're living in the hope of the fullness of that salvation yet to come. Make John's desire your own: "Even so, come, Lord Jesus" (Rev. 22:20).

THE MOTIVE OF THE CHURCH

To Him be glory in the church.

EPHESIANS 3:21

If you were to survey a group of people and ask them to name the primary purpose of the church, you would probably get a variety of answers.

Some might suggest that the church is a place to form friendships with godly people. It's where believers strengthen each other in faith and where love is cultivated and shared.

Others might suggest that the mission of the church is teaching the Word, training believers for various responsibilities, and instructing children and young people with the purpose of helping them mature in Christ.

Still others might say that another purpose of the church is to praise God. The church is a community of praise that exalts God for who He is and what He has done. Some would suggest that since praise is the central activity of heaven, it must also be the primary responsibility of those on earth.

But as important as fellowship, teaching, and praise are, the primary motive of the church is to glorify God. The apostle Paul described salvation as being "to the praise of the glory of his grace" (Eph. 1:6).

OUR MISSION

*God was in Christ
reconciling the world unto himself.*

2 CORINTHIANS 5:19

 God loved a lost world and sought to win sinners to Himself for His own glory. Christ came into the world out of love and sought to win sinners for the Father's glory. As believers we also are to go to the world in love and to seek to reach the lost for the glory of God. Thus our mission is the same as God's.

We are an extension of the ministry of God the Father and Son in receiving glory by the salvation of lost sinners. Jesus said, "As thou hast sent me into the world, even so have I also sent them into the world" (John 17:18). "As" conveys intention. As the Father sent the Son into the unredeemed world, so the Son has sent believers. Wonder of wonders, we have the privilege of participating in Jesus Christ's mission to a lost world!

THE PREREQUISITE
FOR SUCCESS

*For the Son of Man has come
to seek and to save that which was lost.*

LUKE 19:10

S. D. Gordon wrote a book entitled *Quiet Talks with World Winners*. In it, he tells the story of a group of people who were preparing to ascend Mount Blanc in the Swiss Alps. The guides explained that because of the extreme difficulty of the climb, each person should take only necessary climbing equipment, leaving behind all personal accessories.

A young Englishman ignored the advice and brought extra items, but on the way to the summit, he left them behind, one at a time. Finally, when he had reached the top, he had jettisoned everything except the essential equipment.

S. D. Gordon made this application to the Christian life: "Many of us, when we find we can't make it to the top with our loads, let the top go, and pitch our tents in the plain, and settle down with our small plans and accessories. The plain seems to be quite full of tents" (55). The question we must all ask ourselves is, *Are my personal accessories preventing me from fulfilling the mission God has given me?*

ARE YOU AVAILABLE?

Here am I! Send me.

ISAIAH 6:8

God desires a heart that is available at the appointed place and time to hear His orders. He also desires a heart full of true worship. The believer's whole affection and mind is to be set on Christ. All his goals are directed toward Him. He is his all in all.

So are you available? Are you a worshiper? Is your intent and purpose in life focused on the Person of Christ? Having those attitudes means being controlled by the Holy Spirit, who is the only One who can cause you to call Jesus Lord (1 Cor. 12:3). All your possessions, time, energy, talent, and gifts are to be under His control.

That also means being centered on the Word because the Word is where Christ is seen. You gaze at His glory in the Word. As Christ came into the world to give His life to bring people to Himself, so you must do likewise.

ALL AUTHORITY

All authority has been given
to Me in heaven and on earth.

MATTHEW 28:18

Before Christ issued the Great Commission, to "make disciples of all the nations," He had to establish His divine authority to give it. Otherwise, the command would have seemed impossible to fulfill.

As the disciples followed Jesus for three and a half years, they learned much about His authority. He showed them that He had authority over sickness (Matt. 4:23) and death (John 11:43–44). He gave His disciples the same power He had to overcome disease and demons (Matt. 10:1). He established that He had the authority to forgive sins (Matt. 9:6) and judge all men (John 5:25–29). And He proved that He had the authority to lay down His life and take it up again (John 10:18).

Submission to that absolute authority of Christ is not an option—it is your supreme obligation.

AN ALTERNATE CHOICE

I am not ashamed of the gospel of Christ;
for it is the power of God unto salvation to
everyone that believeth; to the Jew first.

ROMANS 1:16

Before God sent His Son to earth, God's design was to reach the world through Israel, but Israel was unbelieving. Their unbelief is described in a parable about a king who arranged a wedding feast for his son and called for his invited guests (Israel). When the guests refused to come—some were indifferent and others hostile—the king said to his servants, "Therefore go into the highways, and as many as you find, invite to the wedding" (Matt. 22:9). Jesus used this parable to describe apostate Israel, who refused their Messiah and forfeited the celebration planned for them.

God then gave the invitation to another group: the Gentiles. God chose a small group of people gathered on a hillside in Galilee and a few other disciples in Jerusalem to reach the lost world. Through them He would do the work that the nation of Israel had refused to do, and we are called to continue that work.

THE FIRST STEP

*Baptizing them in the name of the Father
and of the Son and of the Holy Spirit.*
MATTHEW 28:19

Baptism is the outward sign of one's inward faith in Christ. It's an act of obedience by which a person demonstrates the reality of his salvation. Salvation is not visibly seen but is a supernatural, spiritual transaction. The fruit or result of salvation, however, should be evident.

In the early church, the initial fruit of obedience was baptism, and this same fruit can be expected today. It's the means by which an individual testifies to his or her union in the death, burial, and resurrection of Christ (Rom. 6:3–4). Galatians 3:27 says, "As many of you as have been baptized into Christ have put on Christ."

The Great Commission in Matthew 28 commands us to preach the gospel and baptize others. That means we're to tell people that salvation is something they should not only believe, but also publicly confess, with baptism as the first step. When someone is reluctant to publicly confess Christ in that way, we have reason to question the genuineness of his faith. Jesus said, "Whoever confesses Me before men, him I will also confess before My Father who is in heaven" (Matt. 10:32). That is the public confession we all should make.

THE LOST SHEEP

There will be more joy in heaven over
one sinner who repents than over ninety-nine
just persons who need no repentance.

LUKE 15:7

At the beginning of the parable of the lost sheep, Jesus asks, "What man of you, having a hundred sheep, if he loses one of them, does not leave the ninety-nine in the wilderness, and go after the one which is lost until he finds it?" (Luke 15:4). Jesus' point is that any shepherd would seek a lost sheep, for it is not only a matter of duty but also of affection.

After finding the one sheep, the shepherd in this parable went home and invited people over to celebrate with him. The shepherd's joy was so great he had to share it.

Today's verse is the conclusion to this parable and a hope for Christians today. Just as a shepherd rejoices over the lost sheep, our Great Shepherd rejoices over the repentant sinner, for He has found His lost sheep.

MARCH 19

RENEWING OUR PASSION

Jesus went about all the cities and villages,
teaching in their synagogues,
preaching the gospel of the kingdom.
MATTHEW 9:35

Everything worthwhile in life is the result of someone's passion. Significant events of human history are the result of a deep and consuming desire to see goals fulfilled. The consuming desire of believers should be to see the gospel reach the world. However, we live in an age that tends to dull our sharpness. Our culture obscures legitimate goals and would rob our faith of its fiery power if given the chance.

Indeed, some Christians are a cold bath for the fiery heart. They just don't understand someone with a passionate concern about a spiritual enterprise, because spiritual passion is not the norm. The norm is not to let Christianity disrupt your lifestyle. If you follow that, your spiritual temperature will drop and you'll become apathetic.

We all need to ask ourselves, *Where is our burden for evangelism? Why isn't evangelism the church's central function? Is the church only a self-indulgent activity center, content with comfort and prosperity?*

EXAMPLES OF PASSION

He Himself gave some to be apostles, some prophets,
some evangelists, and some pastors and teachers.

EPHESIANS 4:11

It was said that John Wesley did more for England than her armies and navies. He lived meagerly, having given away thousands of dollars in his lifetime. Abused and maligned, he left his reputation and soul in the hands of God. It has been estimated he traveled 225 thousand miles on foot and horseback and preached twenty-four hundred sermons. Much of the established church despised him, but he brought fire into her cold heart. He had the reputation of being out of breath pursuing souls.

Ordained at twenty-two, George Whitefield began preaching with tremendous eloquence and effect. His power came from his passion for souls, and he used every one of his God-given abilities to lead men to Christ. He crossed the Atlantic thirteen times and preached thousands of sermons. His gravestone reads that he was a soldier of the cross, humble, devout, and ardent, preferring the honor of Christ to his own interest, reputation, or life.

Though these men are wonderful examples, the perfect example of One with passion for the lost is Christ.

Grieving Over Lost Souls

*How often I wanted to gather your
children together, as a hen gathers her chicks
under her wings, but you were not willing!*

Matthew 23:37

Jesus deeply cared for individuals. Our Lord brought Philip (John 1:43), Matthew (Matt. 9:9), and Peter and Andrew (Matt. 4:18–19) to faith with the call, "Follow Me." In John 4, He met a woman at a well and brought her to salvation. In Luke 19, He found Zaccheus, a tax collector, whom He led to a confession of sin, repentance, and faith. In John 3, He taught Nicodemus about the new birth. In Mark 10, He led blind Bartimaeus to believe in Him. In Mark 5, Jesus healed a demon-possessed man in the country of the Gerasenes. And Luke 23 tells of His brief yet poignant encounter with the thief on the cross (vv. 40–43); before committing Himself to God, Christ rescued him from eternal hell.

Jesus' heart grieved over the souls of lost men and women. In John 5:40, we see a glimpse of Christ's passion when He said, "You are unwilling to come to Me that you may have life." There's a pensive quality to those words. Does your heart echo the affection of his speech?

THE MODEL OF WITNESSING

Imitate me, just as I also imitate Christ.

1 CORINTHIANS 11:1

Christ is the perfect model to imitate in witnessing to others. First, He was available. Although there were times when He left the crowds, Jesus was regularly among the people, even when He was busy.

Second, He wasn't partial. Often Jesus was with common people, lepers, prostitutes, and tax collectors—those belonging to the lower classes socially and morally. But He also helped a Roman centurion, a man of dignity and stature (Matt. 8:5–13), and ministered to wealthy Jairus, whose daughter needed a miracle (Mark 5:22–24, 35–43). Jesus reflected the mind of God, who is no respecter of persons (Acts 10:34).

Third, He was sensitive to the pain of others. In Mark 5, a lady with a hemorrhage for twelve years reached out and touched Christ's garment. Jesus asked, "Who touched My garments?" (v. 30) out of concern for her.

Last, He secured a public confession from those who believed in Him, such as the blind man (John 9:1–41), and the Samaritan leper (Luke 17:11–19).

Follow Christ's example as you witness to others.

FISHING FOR MEN

Follow Me, and I will make you fishers of men.

MATTHEW 4:19

Fishermen in the first century used special tools for catching fish. One was a line and hook (Matt. 17:27). Another was a spear or possibly a type of harpoon (Job 41:26). A third was the dragnet (Matt. 13:47). It was sometimes over three hundred feet long and about eight feet wide. Fishermen buoyed up one side with corks and weighed down the other side with lead sinkers. Sometimes they stretched the net between two boats and rowed in a circle. They would then draw in ropes attached to the bottom of the net, trapping the fish (John 21:6).

In today's verse, however, Jesus was referring to a casting net, which had a circular form (about fifteen feet in diameter) made of fine mesh and lead sinkers around the edge. Attaching a long piece of line to the center of the net, the fisherman would cast it into shallow water. He then would draw up the center of the net by its cord and wade into the water to secure the catch.

Just as the disciples caught a school of fish within the reaches of their circular net, the Lord wants His contemporary disciples to reach out to the men and women around us.

FEEDING YOUR PASSION

He was moved with compassion for them,
because they were weary and scattered,
like sheep having no shepherd.

MATTHEW 9:36

How can you enhance your passion for the lost? First, study Christ's great love, compassion, and tender mercy. You can study great men and women in church history, but ultimately you must understand the heart of Jesus. As 1 John 2:6 says, "He who says he abides in Him ought himself also to walk just as He walked."

Second, study sin: its guilt, power, and penalty. That will make you aware of how we have all fallen prey to the subtleties of the world. Romans 12:2 says, "Do not be conformed to this world, but be transformed by the renewing of your mind." Let it remind you to be preoccupied not with worldly things, but with evangelizing the lost.

Third, study sinners. Try to cultivate love and sympathy for them, not bitterness. Note that the most zealous evangelists are often new converts.

Fourth, study Scripture. See what it says about hell, death, judgment, and salvation.

And finally, pray for God to give you a passion for evangelism.

CATCH THE TIDE

Lift up your eyes and look at the fields,
for they are already white for harvest.

JOHN 4:35

All believers are responsible to have a passion for the lost. John Harper had such a passion. He was a newly called pastor to the great Moody Memorial Church in Chicago in the early 1900s, but in 1912 He was a passenger on the ill-fated voyage of the *Titanic*.

Four years later, a young Scotsman rose up in a meeting and said he was a survivor of the Titanic. As he drifted in the water on a piece of wood, he encountered a man who was afloat on a piece of wreckage. The man pleaded for the Scotsman to receive Christ. The young Scotsman refused. The tide brought the man around again, and he asked if the Scotsman was saved yet. Shortly after, the man disappeared into the water, and the Scotsman decided to trust Christ as Savior. At the meeting he identified the man as John Harper—the young Scotsman was John Harper's last convert.

Can you be one of the John Harpers of this generation?

GLORY THROUGH SUFFERING

For our light affliction,
which is but for a moment, is working for us a
far more exceeding and eternal weight of glory.

2 CORINTHIANS 4:17

Suffering not only makes us stronger now—it makes us able to endure with patience, increases our faith, teaches us to trust God, and leads us to depend on Christ and His Word—but also affects how we will function later. That's why Paul went on to say our focus isn't on today but the future: "We do not look at the things which are seen, but at the things which are not seen. For the things which are seen are temporary, but the things which are not seen are eternal" (v. 18).

The greater our endurance through suffering, the greater our eternal reward.

IDENTIFYING WITH CHRIST'S SUFFERING

It was fitting for Him, for whom are all things and by whom are all things, in bringing many sons to glory, to make the captain of their salvation perfect through sufferings.

HEBREWS 2:10

 Christians can identify with their Master because like Him, they suffer to enter their glory.

Christ said to the disciples on the road to Emmaus, "O foolish ones, and slow of heart to believe in all that the prophets have spoken! Ought not the Christ to have suffered these things and to enter into His glory?" (Luke 24:25–26). Our Lord had to explain that future glory required that He suffer. We should expect the same.

The path to glory for Christ was the path of unjust suffering. That's our path also. Jesus endured suffering with perfect patience and was exalted to the highest point of glory. He is our example of how to respond to suffering.

THE TRUE PICTURE

*I determined not to know anything
among you except Jesus Christ and Him crucified.*

1 CORINTHIANS 2:2

Jesus Christ evokes many images in the minds of people. Some picture Him as a baby in a manger—the Christ of Christmas. Others picture Him as a child, perhaps living in the home of a carpenter or confounding the religious leaders of Jerusalem. Many picture Him as a compassionate and powerful healer who restored the sick and raised the dead. Still others picture a bold and fiery preacher speaking the Word of God to great crowds. And there are those who see Him as the consummate man—a model of goodness, kindness, sympathy, concern, care, tenderness, forgiveness, wisdom, and understanding.

Yet the one image of Christ that surpasses all the rest is Jesus Christ on the cross. To know Christ crucified is to know Him as the author and finisher of your faith—the truest picture of His Person and work.

Christ's suffering on the cross is the focal point of the Christian faith. That's where His deity, humanity, work, and suffering are most clearly seen.

A SUFFERING STANDARD

For such a High Priest was fitting for us,
who is holy, harmless, undefiled, separate from sinners,
and has become higher than the heavens.

1 PETER 3:18

Jesus was executed as a criminal on a cross. Yet He was guilty of no crime—no wrong, no trespass, no sin. He never had an evil thought or spoke an evil word. His was the most unjust execution ever perpetrated on a human being. Yet it shows us that though a person may be perfectly within the will of God—greatly loved and gifted, perfectly righteous and obedient—he may still experience unjust suffering. Like Jesus, you may be misunderstood, misrepresented, hated, persecuted, and even murdered. Yet you must follow His standard.

FOLLOW CHRIST'S EXAMPLE

Christ also suffered for us,
leaving us an example,
that you should follow His steps.

1 PETER 2:21

Jesus gave us the ultimate example of suffering. The Greek word translated as "example" refers to a pattern that is placed under a piece of paper to be traced. Like children who learn their letters using tracing paper over a pattern, we are to trace our lives according to the pattern Christ laid down for us.

We follow His pattern by walking "in His steps." We are to walk in Christ's steps because His was a righteous walk. It was also a walk of unjust suffering, which is part of the walk of righteousness. Some suffer more than others, but if you truly want to follow after Christ, you will practice tracing His example.

Our Sinless Savior

[Christ] committed no sin,
nor was deceit found in His mouth;
who when He was reviled,
did not revile in return.

1 Peter 2:22–23

Jesus would have been prominent in Peter's mind when he wrote today's verses because he personally witnessed Jesus' pain—though from afar. In spite of the severity of His pain, however, Christ committed no sin in word or deed.

Isaiah 53:9 says, "He had done no violence." "Violence" is translated as "lawlessness" in the Septuagint (the Greek version of the Hebrew Old Testament). The translators understood that "violence" referred to violence against God's law—or sin. In spite of the unjust treatment He had to endure, Christ did not and could not sin (cf. 1 Pet. 1:19).

Isaiah 53:9 adds, "Nor was any deceit in His mouth." Sin usually first makes its appearance in us by what we say. In Jesus there was no sin, neither externally nor internally.

Jesus Christ is the perfect model of how we are to respond to unjust treatment because He endured far worse treatment than any person who will ever live, and yet never sinned.

Triumph

APRIL

No Striking Back

He was oppressed and He was afflicted, yet He opened not His mouth; He was led as a lamb to slaughter, and as a sheep before its shearers is silent, so He opened not His mouth.

ISAIAH 53:7

Jesus reflects a humble attitude before His tormentors: "When He was reviled, did not revile in return" (1 Pet. 2:23). Though under sustained provocation, Jesus spoke no evil because there was no sin in His heart.

However, under similar provocation, our reaction would be more like that of the apostle Paul's. When he was on trial before the Sanhedrin, the high priest Ananias ordered him to be struck on the mouth. His immediate response to Ananias was, "God will strike you, you whitewashed wall!" (Acts 23:3). Paul immediately had to apologize—such an exclamation against a high priest was against the law (vv. 4–5; cf. Ex. 22:28).

Paul wasn't perfect. He is not our standard of righteousness. Only Christ is a perfect standard of how to handle the reviling of one's enemies.

Like our Master, we are never to abuse those who abuse us.

DON'T THREATEN

Father, forgive them,
for they do not know what they do.

LUKE 23:35

Jesus "did not threaten" in the face of incredible suffering (1 Pet. 2:23). He was spit on, His beard was pulled out, a crown of thorns was crushed onto His head, and nails were driven through His flesh to pin Him to a cross. In any other person, such unjust treatment would have caused feelings of retaliation to well up and burst out, but not Christ. He was the Son of God—creator and sustainer of the universe, holy and sinless—with the power to send His tormentors into eternal flames.

Yet Jesus never threatened His executioners with impending judgment; instead He forgave them. Christ died for sinners, including those who persecuted Him. He knew the glory of salvation could be reached only through the path of suffering, so He accepted His suffering without bitterness, anger, or a spirit of retaliation. May you respond as well to your suffering.

Let God Handle It

Father, into Your hands I commit My spirit.

Luke 23:46

The apostle Peter instructed Christians not to be "returning evil for evil or reviling for reviling, but on the contrary blessing" (1 Pet. 3:9). That was Jesus' attitude. He was able to do that because He "committed Himself to Him who judges righteously" (2:23). The word translated as "committed" means "to hand over for someone to keep." In every instance of suffering, our Lord handed over the circumstance and Himself to God. That's because He was confident in the righteous judgment of God and the glory that would be His. That confidence allowed Him to accept tremendous suffering calmly.

That's the way you should respond when confronted with unjust persecution on the job or in your families or other relationships. When you retaliate, you forfeit the blessing and reward that suffering is meant to bring. Retaliation shows you lack the confidence you ought to have in God's ability to make things right in His own time, which will include punishing the unjust and rewarding those who are faithful in suffering. So give it over to God and let Him handle it.

VINDICATED

Lord, do not charge them with this sin.

ACTS 7:60

We live in a day when Christianity is becoming increasingly unpopular with secular society. Strong stands for the truth of Scripture and the gospel message may soon become intolerable. That will result in the unjust treatment of Christians.

The prospect of such treatment ought to drive us to passages like 1 Peter 2:21–25 for reassurance. There we learn that like our Lord, we are to walk the path of suffering to attain the glory of reward and exaltation in the future. That realization surely prompted Stephen to fix his eyes on Jesus in glory and ask God to forgive his murderers (Acts 7:54–60). He entrusted Himself to God, knowing that He would vindicate him. If you do the same, God will also vindicate you.

OUR SUBSTITUTE

[He] Himself bore our sins in His own body on the tree,
that we, having died to sins, might live for righteousness—
by whose stripes you were healed.

1 PETER 2:24

The substitutionary death of Jesus Christ is an essential truth of the Christian faith. Redemption, justification, reconciliation, removal of sin, and propitiation are all corollaries of Christ's substitutionary work.

The apostle Paul also emphasized this work when he said that God "made Him who knew no sin to be sin for us, that we might become the righteousness of God in Him" (2 Cor. 5:21), and that "Christ has redeemed us from the curse of the law, having become a curse for us"(Gal. 3:13).

Some claim it's immoral to teach that God would take on human flesh and bear the sins of men and women in their stead. They say it's unfair to transfer the penalty of sin from a guilty person to an innocent person. But that's not what happened. Christ willingly took on our sin and bore its penalty. If He had not willed to take our sin and accept its punishment, as sinners we would have borne the punishment of sin in hell forever. Christ's work on the cross wasn't unfair— it was God's love in action!

THE WEIGHT
OF OUR PENALTY

Christ was offered once to bear the sins of many.

HEBREWS 9:28

When the apostle Peter said that Christ "bore" our sins (1 Pet. 2:24), he used a term that means "to carry a massive, heavy weight." That's what sin is. It's so heavy that Romans 8:22 says, "The whole creation groans and labors" under its weight. Only Jesus could remove such a weight from us.

When Christ "bore our sins," He bore the penalty for our sins. He endured physical and spiritual death. When Jesus cried out on the cross, "My God, My God, why have You forsaken Me?" (Matt. 27:46), His was the cry of spiritual death. That was the penalty for bearing our sins.

The Transformation

We also should walk in newness of life.

ROMANS 6:4

The purpose for Jesus' substitutionary sacrifice was that "we, having died to sins, might live for righteousness" (1 Pet. 2:24). Peter doesn't say Christ died so we could go to heaven, have peace, or experience love. He died to bring about a transformation: to make saints out of sinners. Christ's substitutionary work enables a person to depart from sin and enter into a new life pattern: a life of righteousness.

The apostle Paul said, "Our old man was crucified with Him, that the body of sin might be done away with, that we should no longer be slaves of sin" (Rom. 6:6). We have died to sin; thus it no longer has a claim on us. First Peter 2:24 echoes that thought: our identification with Christ in His death is a departure from sin and a new direction in life.

CHRIST OUR SHEPHERD

You were like sheep going astray,
but have now returned to the Shepherd
and Overseer of your souls.

1 PETER 2:25

Today's verse is the apostle Peter's allusion to Isaiah 53:6, which says, "All we like sheep have gone astray; we have turned, every one, to his own way; and the Lord has laid on Him the iniquity of us all." If the Lord had not provided a sacrifice for sin, He could never have brought us into His fold.

The task of a shepherd is to guard sheep. The Greek term for "shepherd" in 1 Peter 2:25 can also be translated as "pastor." That, along with the word translated as "overseer," describes the responsibilities of elders (cf. 1 Pet. 5:2). Jesus guards, oversees, leads, and supervises His flock. He said, "The good shepherd gives His life for the sheep" (John 10:11). That's exactly what He did to bring us to Himself.

OVERCOMING THROUGH SUFFERING

They overcame him [Satan] by the blood
of the Lamb and by the word of their testimony,
and they did not love their lives to the death.

REVELATION 12:11

Christians are aliens and strangers in the world, waging war against fleshly lusts and being slandered and persecuted. As a result, we must expect to suffer in the name of the One who endured all manner of suffering for us (1 Pet. 2:11–25). The central thrust of Peter's message is to remind us of the necessity of suffering. When in the midst of suffering we sin in thought, word, or deed by retaliating, we lose our victory and damage our testimony.

According to today's verse, you overcome the insults, persecutions, and accusations of Satan by the blood of the Lamb, our Savior. That's the power of God. You're an overcomer when you don't lose your testimony by retaliating during times of persecution, and when you don't compromise—even to the point of death. Are you willing to stand strong in the suffering?

LIVING IN A HOSTILE WORLD

Having your conduct honorable among the Gentiles,
that when they speak against you as evildoers,
they may, by your good works which they observe,
glorify God in the day of visitation.

1 PETER 2:12

You may not have realized it before, but living as a Christian in this world is like being a foreigner without a permanent home or citizenship. The apostle Peter referred to believers as "sojourners and pilgrims" (1 Pet. 2:11). You should consider yourself as a temporary citizen and abstain from participating in the world's ungodliness.

That's an important perspective to maintain as hostility toward Christianity mounts in our society. Many unbelievers treat immorality as an alternative lifestyle and believe man can solve his problems any way he chooses.

To live in such a society, you need to arm yourself with a trust in the power of righteousness to triumph over persecution and suffering. During times of hostility, you're to have confidence and not get caught up in turmoil.

A PASSION FOR GOODNESS

Who is he who will harm you
if you become followers of what is good?
1 PETER 3:13

Most people find it difficult to mistreat those who are fervent in doing good. Those who love to do good are often gracious, unselfish, kind, loving, and caring. But frauds who steal from widows and orphans are not tolerated. Even the ungodly condemn those who make themselves rich at the expense of others.

A person who is generous and thoughtful toward others usually isn't the object of hostility. That's Peter's point in today's verse. Peter wanted all his readers to zealously pursue doing good. A passion for doing good produces a pure life, which should be the goal and delight of every believer. When you are consumed with godly living, you will lose any appetite for the world's ungodly attractions.

LEAVING NO CAUSE

But even if you should suffer for
righteousness' sake, you are blessed.

1 PETER 3:15

 It's not likely, but according to the apostle Peter, there is a remote possibility that you may suffer for being righteous. Indeed, many Christians suffered for their obedience to Christ in the early church, but others suffered for their disobedience. When a Christian disobeys God's Word, the world senses a greater justification and freedom for hostility. Even godly Christians should not be surprised or afraid when the world treats them with hostility.

A passion for goodness is no guarantee against persecution. Doing good only reduces the likelihood of it. No one did more good than Jesus, yet a hostile world eventually killed Him. Nevertheless, your life should be above reproach so critics will have no justification for any accusations against you.

A HELPFUL FEAR

You are not to fear what they fear or be in dread of it.
It is the Lord of hosts whom you should regard as holy.
And He shall be your fear, and He shall be your dread.

ISAIAH 8:12–13, NASB

In the days of the prophet Isaiah, Ahaz king of Judah faced a crisis in the impending invasion of the Assyrian army. When Ahaz refused an alliance with the kings of Israel and Syria against Assyria, they also threatened to invade Judah. Behind the scenes Ahaz had allied with Assyria. Isaiah warned Ahaz against that ungodly alliance, but told him not to fear. The king was only to fear the Lord and not be troubled.

In the same sense, a Christian is not to be shaken by whatever hostilities threaten him. Fearing the Lord will help him face opposition with courage and see suffering as an opportunity for spiritual blessings, not as an opportunity to compromise his faith before the believing world.

To be dedicated to the Lord in the face of persecution demands that your mind and affections be set on heavenly values, not earthly ones. If you're preoccupied with possessions, pleasures, and popularity, you'll fear the enemy's assaults. But if you're heavenly minded, you'll rejoice when you encounter various trials.

DEVOTION TO CHRIST

Sanctify the Lord God in your hearts.

1 PETER 3:15

 Regardless of the opposition a believer may face in this world, he is always to affirm in his heart that Christ is Lord. He is to accept and acknowledge the Lord's sovereignty and majesty, fearing only Him.

The believer who sanctifies Christ exalts Him as the object of his love and loyalty. He recognizes His perfection, magnifies His glory, and extols His greatness. He submits himself to God's will, realizing that His will sometimes involves suffering. To live that way is to "adorn the doctrine of God our Savior in all things" (Titus 2:10).

As a Christian, you need to be committed to honoring Christ as Lord—even in the midst of suffering. Submission to Him will yield courage, boldness, and fortitude in the midst of hostility.

DEFENDING THE FAITH

Always be ready to give a defense to
everyone who asks you a reason for the hope
that is in you, with meekness and fear.

1 PETER 3:15

When society attacks, you need to be ready to make a defense. The Greek term for "defense" often referred to a formal defense in a court of law. But Paul also used the word informally to describe his ability to answer *anyone* who questioned him—not just a judge, magistrate, or governor (Phil. 1:16–17). Furthermore, including the word *always* in today's verse indicates that you should be prepared to answer in all situations, not just the legal sphere.

Whether in an official setting or informally to anyone who might inquire, you need to be ready to provide an answer about "the hope that is in you" (1 Pet. 3:15)—that is, give a description of your Christian faith. You should be able to give a rational explanation of your salvation.

A TENDER RESPONSE

*A servant of the Lord must
not quarrel but be gentle to all.*

2 TIMOTHY 2:24

A Christian is to explain his faith "with meek-ness and fear" (1 Pet. 3:15). This indicates a tender and gracious spirit in speaking. The kind of fear we ought to have is a healthy devotion to God, a healthy regard for the truth, and a healthy respect for the person we're talking to. That's why you can't be quarrelsome when defending your faith.

A Christian who can't carefully, thoughtfully, reasonably, and biblically give a clear explanation for his faith will be insecure when faced with hostility and might be inclined to doubt his salvation. The enemy's blows will devastate those who haven't put on "the breastplate of faith and love, and as a helmet the hope of salvation" (1 Thess. 5:8).

A PURE CONSCIENCE

Having a good conscience,
that when they defame you as evildoers,
those who revile your good conduct in Christ
may be ashamed.

1 PETER 3:16

The conscience either accuses or excuses a person, acting as a source of conviction or affirmation. A good conscience doesn't accuse a believer of sin because he is living a godly life. Instead, a good conscience affirms that everything is well, while an evil conscience points out sin.

A believer is to live with a clear conscience so that the weight of guilt won't burden him when he faces hostile criticism. However, if he doesn't have a passion for doing good or serving Christ, he will know the heavy weight of deserved guilt. A defiled conscience can't be at ease or withstand the onslaught of trials. But a clear conscience will help you not to be anxious or troubled during your trials.

TRANQUILITY IN CRITICISM

*If you are reproached for
the name of Christ, blessed are you.*

1 PETER 4:14

A pure conscience provides tranquility and vindicates you when you are slandered. It will be free from the task of pointing out any sin, and your godly life will prove any criticisms to be false. When you have a pure conscience, the verbal abuse and insults against you bring shame to your accuser, not you.

The world self-righteously condemns Christianity when it can point to a Christian who has scandalized the faith. Unbelievers enjoy drawing attention to a sinning Christian so they can justify their own sinful behavior. Therefore, live above reproach so that the unbeliever's accusations will be without any foundation.

YOUR TWO OPTIONS

For it is better, if it is the will of God,
to suffer for doing good than for doing evil.

1 PETER 3:17

You have two options. The first is to do right, even if it results in suffering. You then accept suffering as part of God's wise and sovereign plan for your life.

The second option is to do wrong, which also will result in suffering. Both options are available according to God's will. God wills that you suffer for doing right so you will receive spiritual strength and glorify God. But He also wills that you suffer divine chastisement for doing wrong. So do good, and avoid bringing suffering on yourself for all the wrong reasons.

CHRIST'S TRIUMPH

Christ also suffered once for sins,
the just for the unjust, that He might bring us to God.

1 PETER 3:18

It's incredible to think that One who was perfectly just would die for the unjust. Pilate was correct when he said of Jesus, "I find no guilt in this man" (Luke 23:4). The charges brought against our Lord were fabricated. The witnesses were bribed, and the conviction itself was illegal.

Yet Christ triumphed through such unjust suffering by bringing us to God. And though believers will never suffer as substitutes or redeemers, God may use our Christlike response to unjust suffering to draw others to Himself.

So when the Lord asks us to suffer for His sake, we must realize we are only being asked to endure what He Himself endured so that we can point others to Him.

SUFFERING FOR SINS

*For what the law could not do in that it was weak
through the flesh, God did by sending His own Son
in the likeness of sinful flesh, on account of sin.*

ROMANS 8:3

When we as believers suffer persecution, criticism, or even death, we are sinners suffering because of the sins of others. Our pain may come from the sins of hatred, anger, envy, or murder.

Christ also suffered for sins, but as the sinless One. First Peter 2:22 says He "committed no sin." He never thought, said, or did anything evil. Rather, everything He thought, said, and did was perfectly holy. The sins of others placed Him on the cross: of those who mocked Him and those who nailed Him to the cross. He died because of the sins of the whole world.

Today's verse says that Jesus died "on account of sin." He suffered as a sin offering because "the wages of sin is death" (Rom. 6:23). Just as in the Old Testament God required an animal sacrifice to symbolize the need for our atonement for sin, the New Testament presents Christ as *the* sacrifice who provided not a symbol, but the reality of our eternal atonement for sin.

Purposeful Suffering

The forerunner has entered for us,
even Jesus, having become High Priest forever.

HEBREWS 6:20

Christ's purpose in gathering up our sins on the cross and enduring the darkness of death was to open the way to God. The apostle Peter said that Christ died "that He might bring us to God" (1 Pet. 3:18). God demonstrated that truth symbolically by ripping the Temple veil from top to bottom, opening the Holy of Holies to immediate access by all worshipers (Matt. 27:51). As priests, all believers now may come into the presence of God (1 Pet. 2:9; Heb. 4:16).

The Greek verb translated as "He might bring" (1 Pet. 3:18) states the purpose of Jesus' actions. The verb was often used when someone was being introduced. The noun form of the word refers to the one making the introduction. In Jesus' day, officials in the ancient courts controlled the access to the king. Once convinced of a person's right of access, the official would introduce that person into the king's presence. And that's exactly the function Jesus performs for us now. As He said, "No one comes to the Father except through Me" (John 14:6). He came to lead us into the Father's presence.

DRAWN TO CHRIST

No one can come to Me unless
the Father who sent Me draws him;
and I will raise him up at the last day.

JOHN 6:44

Jesus Christ is the One who introduces men and women to God. Those whom He ushers into the Father's presence all have a loathing of their sin, a desire to be forgiven, and a longing to know God. Those attitudes are the work of God in drawing us to Christ. A response to the gospel message thus begins with a change in attitude toward sin and God.

Beyond that initial change in attitude is the transformation brought about in every believer at the instant of salvation. Christ didn't die just to pay the penalty for sin: He died to transform us.

Deserted by most of His followers, Christ hung in darkness and agony on the cross, crying out, "My God, My God, why have You forsaken Me?" (Matt. 27:46). Those were moments that Jesus felt incredible rejection and hostility. Yet out of those very circumstances Christ triumphed by atoning for sin and providing a way for men and women to be introduced to God and transformed. It was a triumph He Himself would soon proclaim (1 Pet. 3:19–20).

A REAL DEATH

Being put to death in the flesh.

1 PETER 3:18

Today's verse indicates that Jesus Christ's physical life ceased. Some dispute the resurrection of Christ from the dead by claiming that He never died but only fainted. Supposedly He was revived by the coolness of His tomb, got up, and walked out. But Peter is clear: Jesus was dead—the victim of a judicial murder.

Christ's Roman executioners made sure He was dead. They broke the legs of the thieves crucified alongside Him to hasten their deaths. (A victim of crucifixion could postpone death as long as he could elevate himself on his legs.) However, they didn't bother to break Christ's legs since they could see He was already dead. To verify His death, they pierced His side, out of which came a flow of blood and water—only blood, not water, would have come out if Jesus had been alive (John 19:31–37). Christ was surely dead. And that means His resurrection was real.

STAYING ALIVE

But made alive in the spirit.

1 PETER 3:18, NASB

Today's verse makes a specific reference to the life of Jesus' spirit—it does not refer to the Holy Spirit. The apostle Peter is contrasting what happened to the flesh (or body) of Jesus with what happened to His spirit. His spirit was alive but His flesh was dead.

Some think "made alive in the spirit" refers to Christ's physical resurrection, but that would necessitate a statement like, "He was put to death in the flesh but made alive in the flesh." The resurrection was a spiritual *and* physical occurrence. Thus Peter's point has to be that though Christ was physically dead, His spirit was still alive.

On the cross, Christ's spirit experienced a brief separation from God. He said, "My God, My God, why have You forsaken Me?" (Matt. 27:46). The separation ended quickly, however, for shortly after our Lord's lament, He said, "Father, into Your hands I commit My spirit" (Luke 23:46). Then, His spirit was no longer separated from God; it was committed to the Father.

PROCLAIMING VICTORY

He went and preached to the spirits in prison.

1 PETER 3:19

Christ went to preach a triumphant sermon before His resurrection Sunday morning. The term for "preached" in today's verse refers to making a proclamation or announcing a triumph. In ancient times, a herald would precede generals and kings in the celebration of military victories, announcing to all the victories that were won in battle.

That's what Jesus went to do—not to preach the gospel but to announce His triumph over sin, death, hell, demons, and Satan. He didn't go to win souls but to proclaim victory over the enemy. In spite of the unjust suffering they subjected Him to, He could declare ultimate victory over sin and death for you and me.

Snatching Victory
from the Jaws of Hell

He shall bruise your head,
and you shall bruise His heel.

Genesis 3:15

Since the beginning of time Satan and his cohorts have been at war with God. We see that cosmic conflict reflected many times in Scripture (e.g., Job 1; Daniel 10:13). After Satan's apparent triumph in bringing about the Fall of mankind, God predicted his eventual destruction by the Messiah, who would triumph ultimately in spite of a seeming setback (Gen. 3:15).

As a result, Satan attempted to destroy the Messianic line by destroying God's people. When that failed, he tried to slaughter the infant Messiah (Matt. 2:16–18). When that didn't work, he attempted to corrupt the Messiah (Matt. 4:1–11). Failure in that attempt caused him to instigate mobs to kill Him. He even tried to make sure the Messiah couldn't come forth from the tomb.

It's been said that hell must have been in the midst of its carnival when Jesus arrived. They were probably celebrating the victory they had tried so hard to secure—but were abruptly disappointed.

ILLUSTRATING SALVATION

[God] waited in the days of Noah,
while the ark was being prepared, in which a few,
that is, eight souls, were saved through water.

Genesis 6:9 through 8:22 tells how Noah and his family were delivered through the Flood. They were the only people who believed God's warning of the coming worldwide catastrophe. As a result, all mankind was drowned in judgment, except them.

Noah preached the righteousness of God for the hundred and twenty years it took him to build the ark. The size of a modern ocean liner (Gen. 6:15), it was sure to attract attention. But it must have been discouraging to build that ark and preach its meaning for over a century, yet have only your immediate family believe.

Noah's tremendous effort was spent on building a vessel he would spend only a year using, but those eight people were safe from God's judgment when it came. The ark served as their shelter from the encompassing judgment of God. What a graphic illustration of salvation!

SAFETY IN CHRIST

There is also an antitype which now saves us—
baptism (not the removal of the filth of the flesh,
but the answer of a good conscience toward God),
through the resurrection of Jesus Christ.

1 PETER 3:21

Just as the Flood immersed everyone but a few in the judgment of God, so the final judgment will fall on all. But those who are in Jesus Christ will pass through judgment safely. Being in Christ is like being in the ark: we ride safely through the storms of judgment.

The baptism Peter refers to in today's verse is qualified by the statement, "not the removal of the filth of the flesh, but the answer of a good conscience toward God." The only baptism that saves a person is one into the death and resurrection of Jesus Christ. Believers go through the death and burial of Christ because of their union with Him, and come out again into the new world of His resurrection.

The ark of Noah was a kind of tomb—those in it died to their old world when they entered it. When they left it, they experienced a resurrection of sorts by entering a new world. That, Peter tells us, is analogous to the experience of every Christian: spiritually we enter Christ and die to the world we come from, and one day we will be resurrected to a new world and life.

A CLEANSED CONSCIENCE

How much more shall the blood of Christ,
who through the eternal Spirit offered Himself
without spot to God, cleanse your conscience from
dead works to serve the living God?

HEBREWS 9:14

Our safety in Christ results from "the answer of a good conscience toward God" (1 Pet. 3:21). The Greek word for "answer" refers to a pledge, in this case agreeing to meet certain conditions required by God before being placed into the ark of safety (Christ).

Unregenerate men and women have consciences that condemn them. One who appeals to God for a good conscience is sick of his sin and desires to be delivered from the load of guilt he bears. He has a crushing and intimidating fear of coming judgment and knows only God can deliver him. He desires the cleansing that comes through the blood of Christ (cf. Heb. 10:22). So he repents of his sin and pleads for forgiveness.

When Christ suffered on the cross, hell threw all its fury at Him, and wicked men vented their hatred on Him. Yet through that suffering, He served as an ark of safety for the redeemed of all ages. And because He triumphantly provided salvation through His suffering, we are safe in Him.

Perseverance

MAY

Reigning Supreme

[Christ] has gone into heaven and is
at the right hand of God, angels and authorities
and powers having been made subject to Him.

1 Peter 3:22

Throughout both the Old and New Testaments, the right hand of God is affirmed as the place of preeminence, power, and authority for all eternity. That's where Jesus went when He had accomplished His work on the cross, and that's where He rules from today.

Romans 8:34 says, "It is Christ who died, and furthermore is also risen, who is even at the right hand of God, who also makes intercession for us." His position at the right hand of God gives Him authority over all created things.

Christ assumed His position of supremacy "after angels and authorities and powers" had been subjected to Him (1 Pet. 3:22)—that is, when Christ declared His triumph to the demons in prison. The cross and the resurrection are what subjected the angelic hosts to Him. When He ascended into heaven, He took His rightful place and is supreme over all.

LEADING US IN TRIUMPH

*Thanks be to God who always leads us
in His triumph in Christ, and through us diffuses
the fragrance of His knowledge in every place.*

2 CORINTHIANS 2:14

There are many possibilities that arise out of unjust suffering for Christ's sake. God may use your suffering to lead someone to Christ. He may use it to help you triumph over demonic persecution, or it may enable another who sees your godly response to persecution to respond in the same way.

Whatever the triumph of your suffering, you may be sure of one thing: if you suffer for Christ's sake, God will lift you up and exalt you into His very presence. Christ will always cause us to triumph even though we suffer unjustly. Don't underestimate the potential of unjust suffering for Christ's sake. So endure whatever suffering comes your way in the light of your coming triumph in Christ!

INTIMATE COMMUNION

My sheep hear My voice,
and I know them, and they follow Me.

JOHN 10:27

The apostle Paul taught the Ephesians that one of the functions of the church is to build up the people in "the knowledge of the Son of God" (4:13). The word *knowledge* refers to full knowledge that is correct and accurate. That is the knowing of which Jesus spoke in today's verse. He was not speaking of merely knowing their identities but of knowing them intimately, and that is the way He wants His people to know Him.

Paul's desire is for every believer to develop this deep knowledge of Christ by building a relationship with Him through prayer and faithful study of and obedience to God's Word. Growing in this deeper knowledge of Christ is a lifelong process that will not be complete until we see the Lord face-to-face.

THE RIGHT RIGHTEOUSNESS

Not having my own righteousness,
which is from the law, but that which
is through faith in Christ.

PHILIPPIANS 3:9

To know Jesus Christ is to have His righteousness, His holiness, and His virtue imputed to us, which makes us right before God.

Throughout his earlier life, the apostle Paul tried to attain salvation through strict adherence to the Law. But when he was confronted by the wondrous reality of Christ, he was ready to trade in all his self-righteous and external morals, good works, and religious rituals for the righteousness granted to him through faith in Christ. Paul was willing to lose the thin and fading robe of his reputation if he could only gain the splendid and incorruptible robe of the righteousness of Christ.

This is the greatest of all benefits because it secures our standing before God. It is God's gift to the sinner, appropriated by faith in the perfect work of Christ, which satisfies God's justice.

MAY 5

RESURRECTION POWER

*That I may know Him
and the power of His resurrection.*

PHILIPPIANS 3:10

Jesus Christ's resurrection most graphically demonstrated the extent of His power. That's the kind of power the apostle Paul wanted to experience because He realized he was helpless to overcome sin on his own.

The resurrection power of Christ deals with sin at our salvation. We experience His resurrection might at salvation. We were buried with Christ in His death, and we rose with Him to "walk in newness of life" (Rom. 6:4).

But to defeat sin daily, we need His resurrection power to be our resource. We need His strength to serve Him faithfully, to conquer temptation, to overcome trials, and to witness boldly. Only as we build our relationship with Christ and tap into His might will we have victory over sin in this life.

ABUNDANT COMFORT

Just as the sufferings of Christ are
ours in abundance, so also our comfort
is abundant through Christ.

2 CORINTHIANS 1:5, NASB

When we suffer, Christ is with us to comfort us during our heartache. The degree to which He has already experienced the same suffering, and even more, is the reason He is able to comfort us.

The test of your character is your response to the severest times of suffering and persecution. When suffering becomes too intense, the easy response is to get angry and blame God. When persecution becomes too severe, the easy way out is to compromise your faith. To respond in either manner will cause you to miss out on the richest fellowship available to you. That's because the deepest moments of spiritual fellowship with the living Christ are the direct result of intense suffering.

Suffering always drives us to Christ because we find in Him our merciful high priest who sympathizes "with our weaknesses" (Heb. 4:15) and who "is able to aid those who are tempted" (2:18). So view your sufferings as opportunities to be blessed by Christ as you find comfort in His fellowship.

THE BLESSINGS OF GROWTH

That they may adorn the doctrine
of God our Savior in all things.

TITUS 2:10

 Since Christians are already entitled to heaven and will attain perfection one day in God's presence, why is spiritual growth necessary? There are a number of reasons.

First, it glorifies God.

Second, it verifies salvation. External change demonstrates an internal change of heart.

Third, it is a good testimony. Spiritual growth puts the truth of God on display for others to see.

Fourth, it provides assurance. When we progress spiritually, we see God at work in our lives, and that helps our confidence in our salvation (2 Pet. 1:10).

Fifth, it spares us unnecessary sorrow. Lack of growth toward godliness results only in pain and sorrow.

Sixth, it protects the cause of Christ from reproach.

And last, it makes us useful for serving in the church.

So continue to grow and be a blessing to those you meet.

Is Perfection Possible?

If we say that we have no sin,
we deceive ourselves.

1 John 1:8

The false doctrine of perfectionism teaches that there is some point following conversion when the believer's sin nature is eradicated. But according to today's verse and especially in the apostle Paul's treatment of the subject in Philippians 3:12–16, perfection in this life is only a goal, not an achievement. We must pursue it, but we'll never attain it while on earth.

Paul denied perfectionism by calling us to pursue a prize that can be fully obtained only in heaven. He confessed that he himself had not reached perfection—and he wrote to the Philippians nearly thirty years after his conversion! He was perhaps the most committed Christian who ever lived. If after thirty years he wasn't perfect, certainly none of us should claim to be.

Not What I Should Be

Not that I have already attained,
or am already perfected.

PHILIPPIANS 3:12

We are not yet what we should be, what we can be, or what we will be when we see the Lord. Our spiritual race begins with a sense of dissatisfaction. Paul started his race with the awareness that he had not arrived.

I can echo Paul's testimony. After many years of walking with the Lord and being involved in ministry, I am acutely aware that I am not what I ought to be. Like every other believer, I am still in the process of growth. People who become content with where they are spiritually have reached a dangerous point. They are probably insensitive to sin and will tend to defend themselves when they should admit their weakness and seek help.

Spiritual growth begins like any race—the runner knows the distance he has to run and puts forth maximum effort right to the finish line. Paul's goal was to become perfect, but knowing he hadn't reached it yet didn't deter him. And neither should it deter you.

MAXIMUM EFFORT

I press on, that I may lay hold of that
for which Christ Jesus has also laid hold of me.

PHILIPPIANS 3:12

Spiritual growth is not an intermittent exercise—it should be all consuming. In fact, the Greek word for "press on" was used to describe a sprinter and speaks of an aggressive, energetic endeavor. Paul was running with all his might, straining every spiritual muscle to win the prize (cf. 1 Cor. 9:24–27). He also said we're to "fight the good fight of faith" (1 Tim. 6:12)

This perspective was not limited to Paul. The author of Hebrews wrote, "Let us lay aside every weight, and the sin which so easily ensnares us, and let us run with endurance the race that is set before us" (Heb. 12:1).

Our lifelong pursuit is to be like Christ. Running that race takes maximum effort using the means of grace God has provided for us.

CONCENTRATE

I do not count myself to have apprehended;
but one thing I do, forgetting those
things which are behind and reaching
forward to those things which are ahead.

PHILIPPIANS 3:13

An athlete running a race must fix his eyes on something ahead of himself. He can't watch his feet or he'll fall on his face. He can't be distracted by the other runners. He must focus on the goal straight ahead.

Paul's remarkable concentration was the result of two things. First, he chose to forget "those things which are behind." That includes both good and bad things. It means we should not dwell on past virtuous deeds and achievements any more than we should think about past sins and failures. Unfortunately, many Christians are so distracted by the past that they don't make any current progress.

Instead of looking at the past, Paul focused on the future. "Reaching forward" pictures a runner stretching every muscle to reach the goal. To do that he has to eliminate the distractions and concentrate only on the goal ahead. Do you have that kind of concentration in your desire to become like Christ?

SPIRITUAL MOTIVATION

I press toward the goal for the prize
of the upward call of God in Christ Jesus.

PHILIPPIANS 3:14

The apostle Paul's goal was to be like Christ. He knew that he would receive his reward when God's upward call came. Like Paul, we won't reach the goal of Christlikeness in this life, but we will receive it instantly in the next: "It has not yet been revealed what we shall be, but we know that when He is revealed, we shall be like Him, for we shall see Him as He is" (1 John 3:2).

The upward call of God is our motivation to run the race. We should live in light of being called out of this world at any time into the presence of God, where we will receive our eternal reward. We were vile, godless sinners on our way to hell when God sovereignly chose us for salvation that He might eternally make us like His own Son. What grace! What motivation to reach for the goal!

DEPENDING ON
DIVINE RESOURCES

Therefore let us, as many as are mature,
have this mind; and if in anything you think otherwise,
God will reveal even this to you.

PHILIPPIANS 3:15

Unfortunately, in every church some Christians are content with their spiritual state. Instead of recognizing their need, they expend their energies justifying the level they have attained.

Today's verse basically says that if some believers don't yet understand the importance of pursuing growth, God will have to reveal it to them. I pour my heart out in my messages, but I realize that some of my listeners will continue to live uncommitted lives. When you reach that point with someone you're ministering to, you just have to ask God to reveal Himself to that individual.

In pursuing Christ, we all need to depend on divine resources. There will be times in the race when you don't have the proper attitude, and God will have to reveal that to you so you can move on.

BE CONSISTENT

Let us keep living by that same
standard to which we have attained.

PHILIPPIANS 3:16, NASB

You can't win a race without a consistent effort because Christlikeness is an ongoing pursuit. The Greek verb for "keep living" speaks of walking in line. Paul was saying that we need to stay in line spiritually, to keep moving forward by the same principles that got us this far.

Are you moving forward? Or are you standing in one place looking backward and defending yourself? Perhaps you need to refresh your commitment. If you don't know Jesus Christ, then you start growing by receiving Him as Lord and Savior. If you do know Him but have not been growing spiritually, ask God to forgive you and help you move toward perfection. May we all be committed to the goal of becoming as much like Christ as we can until we see Him.

UNDERSTANDING OUR GOAL

He who says He abides in Him
ought himself also to walk just as He walked.

1 JOHN 2:6

The Christian life is simply the process of pursuing Christ's likeness, theologically described as sanctification. Jesus said, "Follow Me," and that simple command has not been replaced or improved on. Following Christ involves learning from Him so we can be like Him (Luke 6:40). Romans 8:29 says God saved us so that we can become "conformed to the image of His Son." Therefore, our one pursuit is to become more and more like Christ.

Now some people may argue that glorifying God or evangelizing the lost are more important priorities. But being like Christ glorifies God, and if we are like Christ we can't help but reach out to others. After all, He came "to seek and to save that which was lost" (Luke 19:10). All that is needed in the Christian life will flow out of a pursuit of Christlikeness.

HE'S IN THE BOOK

*As newborn babes, desire the pure milk
of the word, that you may grow thereby.*

1 PETER 2:2

 To become more like Christ you need to know the Word of God. You need to know how Christ lived when He was on earth, and the only place to learn that is the Scriptures, which are the revelation of Christ. The Old Testament sets the scene for Him, creates the need for Him, and predicts His coming. The gospels record His arrival. The Book of Acts describes the immediate impact of His ministry. The epistles delineate the long-term significance of His life and ministry. And Revelation details His future return and judgment of earth.

Christ is the focus of the entire Bible, and you need to study it to know what He is like. Too often we study the Bible for the sake of theological arguments or to answer questions. Those things are important, but the main point of Bible study is to know more about Christ so that you can be like Him.

ALL WE NEED

The kingdom of heaven is like treasure hidden in a field,
which a man found and hid; and for joy over it he goes and
sells all that he has and buys that field.

MATTHEW 13:44

The apostle Paul lived a complex life before he became a Christian (Phil. 3:4–6). He tried to keep all the laws and traditions of Judaism. He tried to accomplish various works that he hoped would be credited to his account. But in all his pursuits, he was seeking something he couldn't find. Then one day, on the road to Damascus, he was confronted by the living Christ and realized He was everything Paul had been looking for.

Paul describes the exchange that was made: "What things were gain to me, these I have counted loss for Christ. Yet indeed I also count all things loss for the excellence of the knowledge of Christ Jesus my Lord, for whom I have suffered the loss of all things, and count them as rubbish, that I may gain Christ" (Phil. 3:7–8). When Paul met Christ, he realized everything in his asset column was actually a liability. He found that Christ was all he needed.

A HELPFUL MOUNTAIN GUIDE

Therefore I urge you, imitate me.

1 CORINTHIANS 4:16

Since all Christians are imperfect, we need the example of someone who also is imperfect but knows how to deal with imperfection. Perhaps this illustration will help. Suppose I decide to embark on a dangerous mountain-climbing expedition. A helicopter drops a leader on top of the mountain, and he looks down on me and says, "This is the top. Just climb up here—this is where you want to be." He would not be as much help as someone climbing up the path ahead of me, saying, "Follow me. I know the way up."

Christ shows us the goal we need to achieve, but we also need someone to model the process of reaching the goal. Only by overcoming sin can we become more like Christ, so we need to find another Christian who is also battling to overcome sin. A godly human example can show you how to deal with all of the products of our fallen flesh. Begin to search for and follow a godly guide.

AN EXCELLENT EXAMPLE

Join in following my example.

There is no better historical example of a Christian than the apostle Paul. He's a dominant figure in the New Testament, so we can conclude that God wants us to pattern our lives after him.

Paul is a model of virtue, worship, service, patience, endurance through suffering, victory over temptation, and good stewardship over possessions and relationships. He shows us how a godly man deals with his fallenness—something Christ could never do because He was sinless (Heb. 4:15)

Paul's life is a marvelous pattern for ours. That's why he told the Corinthians, "Imitate me" (1 Cor. 11:1). He also commended the Thessalonians, saying, "You have become followers of us and of the Lord" (1 Thess. 1:6). Paul is my own personal example in ministry. I look at how he handled situations and try to respond the way he did.

GODLY LEADERS

Note those who so walk,
as you have us for a pattern.

PHILIPPIANS 3:17

Godly leaders are vital to the church because we need to see Christianity lived out before us. Paul told Timothy, "Be an example to the believers in word, in conduct, in love, in spirit, in faith, in purity" (1 Tim. 4:12). A spiritual leader must live an exemplary life because he is to show others the path. People can see perfection in Christ and can read about Paul, but they also need someone they can watch and talk to. They need to see virtue, humility, unselfish service, a willingness to suffer, devotion to Christ, courage, and spiritual growth in the life of someone close to them.

A great burden on my heart is that pastors and elders in every church will be the kind of examples God commands them to be. It is extremely important to teach the truth, but it is equally important for that teaching to be undergirded by a virtuous life.

THE FAILURE OF LEADERS

I have no one like-minded,
who will sincerely care for your state.

PHILIPPIANS 2:20

Church history may record ours as the era of disastrous collapse within the leadership of the church. The standards for leadership have been lowered, and many thousands have tragically lost their way.

Where are the godly and truthful men? Where are the humble, unselfish models of virtue? Where are the examples of victory over temptation? Where are those who show us how to pray and overcome trials or adversity?

We have a sick and distorted church because we've lost sight of Christ, His Word, and the Spirit. We've lost sight of our clear pattern for growth in the life of the apostle Paul. And we have tolerated a lower standard for leadership than the Bible allows. The essence of Christianity is becoming more like Christ. Matters such as right relationships, service, and evangelism will be taken care of if we just pursue that one holy goal.

AVOIDING
MAN-CENTERED THEOLOGY

From among yourselves men will rise up,
speaking perverse things, to draw away
the disciples after themselves.

ACTS 20:30

Many forces hinder our understanding of this basic truth: the goal of every Christian's life is to become more like Christ. Humanistic psychology is one such force. It teaches that man exists for his own satisfaction—he must have all his perceived needs and desires met to be happy. As a result, in many churches spiritual growth is often equated with ironing out life's problems and finding personal fulfillment.

That kind of mentality ultimately leads to a man-centered theology, which is diametrically opposed to what the Bible teaches. The goal of salvation and sanctification is that we be conformed to the image of Christ (Rom. 8:29). It's been well said that faith looks out instead of in, and the whole of life falls into line. The more you know Christ and focus on Him, the more the Spirit will make you like Him. But the more you focus on yourself, the more distracted you will be from the proper path.

NO SECRET TO SUCCESS

No one, having put his hand to the plow,
and looking back, is fit for the kingdom of God.
LUKE 9:62

I have never met a successful, influential person in any realm of enterprise who was not committed to reaching goals. The people who influence the world are pursuers, competitors, and winners, preoccupied with goals rather than having their own needs met. All I have learned about the lives of great Christian leaders has made one thing clear: there is no secret to success—they all put out maximum effort to reach spiritual goals and ignore personal satisfaction during the process.

It's amazing to discover what great preachers, theologians, and missionaries have suffered in the process of reaching their goals. They were far more concerned with following Christ than with their own condition. Can you say the same about your own commitment to Christ?

ENEMIES OF THE CROSS

*Many walk, of who I have told you often, and now tell
you weeping, that they are the enemies of the cross of Christ.*

PHILIPPIANS 3:18

 The most dangerous enemies to the cause of
Christ are not those who openly oppose the
gospel, but those who pretend to be friends of Christ,
claim to identify with Him, and in some cases, reach
positions of spiritual leadership.

Being on guard against hidden enemies is a
constant theme in the New Testament. Jesus said,
"Beware of false prophets, who come to you in sheep's
clothing, but inwardly are ravenous wolves" (Matt.
7:15). He also predicted that in the last days "many false
prophets will rise up and deceive many" (Matt. 24:11).

The apostle Paul was constantly dealing with the
influence of false teachers. He warned the Ephesian
elders: "Therefore watch, and remember that for three
years I did not cease to warn everyone night and day
with tears." (Acts 20:31). Do you want to know how
to acquire the ability to discern enemies of the cross?
Know the Word. If you don't know the Word, you are
open to being misled.

SOLDIERS IN A HOLY WAR

Stand therefore,
having girded your waist with truth.

EPHESIANS 6:14

Our society is not conducive for people becoming like Christ. We live in what has been termed a sensate culture because most people are more concerned with pleasant emotions than with productive efforts—they're more into comfort than accomplishment. Such a perspective has affected even the church, which suffers from an appalling apathy. We have forgotten that we are soldiers in a holy war.

As today's verse indicates, the first thing a soldier put on before he went into battle was a belt around his waist. He would tie it as tight as he could and pull the corners of his tunic up through the belt so that he could have complete freedom of movement in hand-to-hand combat. The belt of truthfulness is not a piece of armor, for it cannot protect us directly. But it does indicate that we are to be serious about the battle and devoted to achieving victory.

An Expectation of Heaven

Seek those things which are above,
where Christ is, sitting at the right hand of God.

COLOSSIANS 3:1

The apostle Paul was preoccupied with heaven; he knew few earthly comforts. He was beaten, stoned, left for dead, deprived of necessities, and frequently disappointed by people. But he had no concern for pleasant feelings: he wanted only to live a productive life in pursuit of his heavenly goal.

We must have the same focus if we are going to pursue our heavenly reward. Christ is from heaven and in heaven. Heaven is His place, and because we are His, heaven is our place as well. If we are preoccupied with being like Him, we will naturally be preoccupied with heaven. What happens there should be more important to us than what happens here.

WHERE'S YOUR TREASURE?

Lay up for yourselves treasures in heaven.

MATTHEW 6:20

Leaving this earth and going to heaven is not a popular thought in the contemporary church. The increasing emphasis on success, prosperity, and personal problem-solving reflects our earthbound perspective.

It's also hard for us to comprehend a future heavenly reward. In this materialistic age, we rarely experience delayed gratification. Almost anything we want, we can have immediately. We don't even need money—we can use a credit card. We don't have to build anything—we can buy it. And we don't have to go very far to get it.

The lack of interest in heaven is the other side of the preoccupation with this world. Heaven is virtually ignored by modern evangelicals. There is little preaching or teaching on the subject, but there are mammoth amounts of material available on prospering in this life. To pursue Christ with the same passion as Paul, we must focus on the world to come.

OUR HOME

Our citizenship is in heaven.

PHILIPPIANS 3:20

Christians are not citizens of this world. The Greek word for "citizenship" in today's verse refers to a colony of foreigners. In a secular source, it is used to describe a capital city that kept the names of its citizens on a register. Indeed, we are registered citizens of another place—heaven. Our names are there, our Father is there, our brothers and sisters are there, and our inheritance is there—it is our home.

The Israelites taken into the Babylonian Captivity give us a historical parallel to the contemporary church. Their home was still the Promised Land even though they lived for so many years in a foreign company. But when it came time to return, many had become so entrenched into the Babylonian culture that they didn't want to leave. When the Lord says it's time to go to heaven, we fight it as if it were the worst thing imaginable because this world has become everything to us. That's why we must always be reminded that our citizenship is in heaven.

MOTIVATED BY CHRIST'S RETURN

From which we also eagerly wait for the Savior,
the Lord Jesus Christ.

PHILIPPIANS 3:20

Anticipating Christ's return is the greatest source of spiritual motivation, accountability, and security. It provides tremendous motivation in pursuing Christ because you will want to be ready when He comes. You will want to have been faithful in serving Him. You can find motivation in the hope of one day being rewarded by Christ and hearing, "Well done good and faithful servant. . . . Enter into the joy of your lord" (Matt. 25:23).

Christ's return provides accountability because that's when "each of us shall give account of himself to God" (Rom. 14:12).

And His return will make you secure, knowing that Jesus said, "This is the will of the Father who sent Me, that of all He has given Me I should lose nothing, but should raise it up at the last day" (John 6:39).

A FORETASTE

*Blessed be the God and Father of our
Lord Jesus Christ, who has blessed us with every
spiritual blessing in the heavenly places in Christ.*

EPHESIANS 1:3

Presently we don't live in heaven physically, but in a sense we do live in the heavenly realm. Though we are not in heaven, we are experiencing heavenly life. We have the life of God within us. We are under the rule of a heavenly King, and we obey heaven's laws.

As a result, we experience "a foretaste of glory divine," as Fanny Crosby noted in the hymn "Blessed Assurance." We are living in a new community, enjoying a new fellowship that will fully come to fruition in a place called heaven.

A POWERFUL RETURN

[Christ] will transform our lowly body that it may be conformed to His glorious body, according to the working by which He is able even to subdue all things to Himself.

PHILIPPIANS 3:21

Today's verse assures us that Jesus Christ has the power to do the amazing things He has promised us. Since He can subject the entire universe to His sovereign control, He certainly has enough power to raise our bodies and make us like Him. He has the power to providentially create natural laws and to miraculously overrule them. He has the power to give life and to take it. The apostle Paul said, "Then comes the end, when He delivers the kingdom to God the Father, when He puts an end to all rule and all authority and power. For He must reign till He has put all enemies under His feet" (1 Cor. 15:24–25).

The same power that will recapture the entire fallen universe and give it back to God is what makes it possible for us to become like Christ. Where is your focus? I hope it is on heaven and that you have not been distracted.

Transformation

JUNE

A Change of Nature

If anyone is in Christ, he is a new creation;
old things have passed away; behold,
all things have become new.

2 Corinthians 5:17

When you receive Jesus Christ, are born again, and enter into God's kingdom, you become a totally different individual. The change that occurs when you're saved is more dramatic than the change that will occur when you die because then you already have a new nature and are a citizen of God's kingdom. Death simply ushers you into God's presence.

In his epistles, the apostle Paul says that when God transformed us, He gave us a new will, mind, heart, power, knowledge, wisdom, life, inheritance, relationship, righteousness, love, desire, and citizenship. He called it "newness of life" (Rom. 6:4). Some teach that when a person becomes a Christian, God gives him something new in addition to his old sin nature. But according to the Word of God, we don't receive something new—we ourselves become new!

THE NEW NATURE

*Having been born again, not of corruptible
seed but incorruptible, through the word of God
which lives and abides forever.*

1 PETER 1:23

When we become Christians we are not remodeled, nor are we added to—we are transformed. Christians don't have two different natures; we have one new nature, the new nature in Christ. The old self dies and the new self lives; they do not coexist. Jesus Christ is righteous, holy, and sanctified, and we have that divine principle in us—what Peter called the "incorruptible" seed (1 Pet. 1:23). Thus our new nature is righteous, holy, and sanctified because Christ lives in us (Col. 1:27).

Ephesians 4:24 tells us to "put on the new man," a new behavior that's appropriate to our new nature. But to do so we have to eliminate the patterns and practices of our old life. That's why Paul tells us to "put to death your members which are on the earth: fornication, uncleanness, passion, evil desire, and covetousness" (Col. 3:5).

CONFORMING TO CHRIST

Do not love the world
or the things in the world.

1 JOHN 2:15

As Christians, we are new creations and members of the church of Jesus Christ, and therefore unique. As a result, we should not live like people in the world. The world is proud; we are humble. The world is fragmented; we are united. The world is impotent; we are gifted. The world is hateful; we are full of love. The world doesn't know the truth; we do. If we don't walk any differently from the world, we won't accomplish Christ's goals. If we live like people in the world, we essentially are imitating the dead (Eph. 2:1–5), and that doesn't make sense.

Christians are like a new race. We have a new spiritual, incorruptible seed, and we must live a lifestyle that corresponds to it. We are new creations who have been suited for an eternal existence. As a result, we can discard our old lifestyle and be conformed to the life of Christ.

THINK DIFFERENTLY

*You should no longer walk as the rest
of the Gentiles walk, in the futility of their mind.*

EPHESIANS 4:17

Salvation is—first and foremost—a change of mind. The apostle Paul says to believers, "You have not so learned Christ" (Eph. 4:20). Christianity is cognitive before it is experiential. A person needs to consider the gospel, believe its historic facts and spiritual truths, and then receive Christ as Savior and Lord.

The first step in that process is repentance, which means that you think differently about sin, about God, about Christ, and about your life than you used to think. The Greek word for "repentance" means "to change one's mind." As it is used in the New Testament, it always refers to a change of purpose, specifically a turning from sin.

That change should result in a change of behavior, which also is based on the mind. In today's verse, Paul says that unregenerate people live "in the futility of their mind." Proverbs 23:7 says, "As he thinks in his heart, so is he." So when you think differently, you will act differently.

Living in Light

You are the light of the world.
A city that is set on a hill cannot be hidden.

Matthew 5:14

The apostle Paul looked at the evil pagan world and concluded that its self-centered, useless thinking leads to darkened understanding and a hard heart. That, in turn, leads to insensitivity to sin and shameless behavior, which then leads to unblushing obscenity. And it's not really much different today.

As believers we shouldn't even dabble in any of the evils characteristic of unbelievers. We are to be a light on a hill, separate from the evil around us. We are to be different. A city that's set on a hill can't be hidden. We must stand as salt and light. But if we're corrupted by the system, we become useless.

Our blessed Lord Jesus Christ purchased us at the cost of His own life. He gave us a new nature that is holy, undefiled, and sanctified forever. He simply asks us to live up to what He has given us by discarding our old lifestyle and taking on our new one.

EXAMINE YOURSELF

*Do you not know that friendship with the world is
enmity with God? Whoever therefore wants to be a friend
of the world makes himself an enemy of God.*

JAMES 4:4

Are you still hanging onto the lifestyle you followed before you became a Christian? As today's verse reveals, if you didn't make a conscious effort to cut yourself off from this world when you came to Christ, you have reason to question whether your salvation was genuine.

First John 2:15 says, "Do not love the world or the things in the world. If anyone loves the world, the love of the Father is not in him." When you become a Christian, your desire should be to cut yourself off from the world. Certainly the world will continue to tempt you from time to time, but you're to forsake the devil's evil system.

To say that a person can come to Christ without making a break from the world is a lie. There must be a change of lifestyle! It's not an easy thing to do—Paul commanded us not to live as we did before we came to Christ (Eph. 4:17). But we can live this life because we have a new nature.

JUNE 7

THE IMPORTANCE
OF REPENTANCE

*Repent, and let every one of you be baptized
in the name of Jesus Christ for the remission of sins.*

ACTS 2:38

No one can come to Jesus Christ unless he repents. Jesus began His ministry proclaiming the need for repentance (Matt. 4:17), and both Peter and Paul continued to proclaim it. Repentance is a conscious choice to turn from the world, sin, and evil. It is crucial!

If you came to Jesus Christ thinking all you had to do was believe but didn't have to confess your sin or be willing to cut yourself off from the evil of this world, you have missed the point of salvation. Many people's lives haven't changed at all since they supposedly believed in Christ. For example, some acted immorally and still act immorally. Some committed adultery and continue to commit adultery. And some committed fornication and continue to commit fornication. Yet according to 1 Corinthians 6:9-10, fornicators and adulterers will not inherit the kingdom of God. If you are really saved, you will make a conscious attempt to break away from the things of the world.

A CHRIST-CENTERED LIFE

You have not so learned Christ,
if indeed you have heard Him.

EPHESIANS 4:20–21

As Christians, we are no longer controlled by a self-centered mind; we learn from Christ. Christ thinks for us, acts through us, loves through us, feels through us, and serves through us. The lives we live are not ours but are Christ living in us (Gal. 2:20). Philippians 2:5 says, "Let this mind be in you which was also in Christ Jesus." An unsaved person walks in the vanity of his own mind, but a saved person walks according to the mind of Christ.

God has a plan for the universe, and as long as Christ is working in us, He's working out a part of that plan through us. Paul noted that He "is able to do exceedingly abundantly above all that we ask or think, according to the power that works in us" (Eph. 3:20). Every day should be a fantastic adventure for us because we're in the middle of God's unfolding plan for the ages.

A RENEWED MIND

Be renewed in the spirit of your mind.

EPHESIANS 4:23

When you become a Christian, God gives you a new mind—but you must fill it with new thoughts. A baby is born with a fresh, new mind, and then impressions are made in the baby's mind that determine the course of his or her life. The same thing is true of a Christian. When you enter into God's kingdom, you're given a fresh, new mind. You then need to build the right thoughts into your new mind. That's why Philippians 4:8 says, "Whatever things are true, whatever things are noble, whatever things are just, whatever things are pure, whatever things are lovely, whatever things are of good report, if there is any virtue and if there is anything praiseworthy— meditate on these things." We have a renewed mind, not a reprobate mind.

Instead of having a reprobate, vile, lascivious, greedy, unclean mind, we have a mind filled with righteousness and holiness. And that should naturally characterize the way we live.

A NEW ATTITUDE

Put on the new man which
was created according to God,
in true righteousness and holiness.

EPHESIANS 4:24

When you came to Christ, you acknowledged that you were a sinner and chose to forsake your sin and the evil things of this world. But Satan will dangle the world and its sin in front of you to tempt you to return to it. Paul warns us not to return to it but to put it off and instead, put on righteousness and true holiness.

That's not something you do once; it's something you do every day. One way you do so is described in 2 Timothy 3:16, which says, "All Scripture is given by inspiration of God, and is profitable for doctrine, for reproof, for correction, for instruction in righteousness." If you want to live correctly, expose yourself to the Word of God. It will help you deal with the traces of the world still present in your life.

BE TRUTHFUL

You shall not bear
false witness against your neighbor.

EXODUS 20:16

A Christian should never tell any type of lie. The most familiar kind of lie is saying something that isn't true. But there are other kinds, such as exaggeration. I once heard the story of a certain Christian man who shared a powerful testimony, but one day he stopped reciting it. When asked why, he said that through the years he had embellished it so much he had forgotten what was true and what he'd made up.

Cheating in school, in business, at work, and on your taxes is a form of lying. So is the betrayal of a confidence, flattery, making excuses, and remaining silent when the truth should be spoken. There's no place for lying in the Christian life. We are to tell the truth.

THE IMPORTANCE OF TRUTH

Therefore, putting away lying,
"Let each of you speak truth with his neighbor,"
for we are members of one another.

EPHESIANS 4:25

Why is it so important to tell the truth? Because we are members one of another. When we don't speak the truth with each other, we harm our fellowship. For example, what would happen if your brain told you that cold was hot and hot was cold? When you took a shower, you'd either freeze to death or scald yourself! If your eye decided to send false signals to your brain, a dangerous curve in the highway might appear straight and you would crash. You depend on the honesty of your nervous system and of every organ in your body.

The Body of Christ can't function with any less than that. We cannot shade the truth with others and expect the church to function properly. How can we minister to each other, bear each other's burdens, care for each other, love each other, build up each other, teach each other, and pray for each other if we do not know what is going on in each others' lives? So be honest, "speaking the truth in love" (Eph. 4:15).

RIGHTEOUS ANGER

Be angry, and do not sin.

EPHESIANS 4:26

You might be surprised to hear that there is such a thing as righteous anger—that is, being angry over what grieves God and hinders His causes. But we are not to be so angry that it results in sin.

Don't be angry for your own causes. Don't get angry when people offend you. And don't let your anger degenerate into personal resentment, bitterness, sullenness, or moodiness. That is forbidden. The only justifiable anger defends the great, glorious, and holy nature of our God.

Anger that is selfish, passionate, undisciplined, and uncontrolled is sinful, useless, and hurtful. It must be banished from the Christian life. But the disciplined anger that seeks the righteousness of God is pure, selfless, and dynamic. We ought to be angry about the sin in the world and in the church. But we can't let that anger degenerate into sin.

WORK HARD

Let him who stole steal no longer,
but rather let him labor, working with his hands
what is good, that he may have something
to give to him who has need.

EPHESIANS 4:28

Theft is a common problem in our world. Shoplifting has become such a problem that a significant percentage of the price of commercial items covers the amount lost from stolen goods. Whether grand theft or petty theft, robbing from the store, or stealing money from a rich man or a family member, it is all stealing.

Christians are to "labor," which refers to hard, manual work. Hard work is honorable. As Christians we should work hard so that we will have enough to give to those in need, not so that we will have more of what we don't need. The worldly approach to wealth is to hoard what we acquire. But the New Testament principle is to work hard so we might do good and give to those who have needs.

USELESS SPEECH

Let no corrupt word
proceed out of your mouth.

EPHESIANS 4:29

Rotten fruit smells terrible and is worthless. You don't want to get near it, let alone eat it. The same thing is true of rotten language. Whether it is off-color jokes, profanity, dirty stories, or crude speech, in no way should it characterize a Christian.

Psalm 141:3 tells us how to eliminate such speech: "Set a guard, O Lord, over my mouth; keep watch over the door of my lips." If Jesus Christ is the doorkeeper of your lips, He will be the one to determine what comes out of them.

EDIFYING WORDS

What is good for necessary edification,
that it may impart grace to the hearers.

EPHESIANS 4:29

If you allow Christ to keep watch over your lips, whatever you say should build up others. You should encourage and strengthen others spiritually. Is that what happens when you talk with people? Do they go away built up in Jesus Christ? Mothers, when you are with your children throughout the day, do your words build them up? Fathers, when you take your children out for the day, are your conversations with them edifying and encouraging?

Today's verse also indicates that we should give others "necessary" edification, meaning that our words fit the need. When I was growing up, whenever I would say to my mom, "Do you know what So-and-so did?" she would respond, "Is that necessary to know?" Often what I wanted to say was interesting, but it certainly wasn't necessary.

Finally our speech should "impart grace to the hearers." Do your words bless those who hear them? Is there graciousness in what you say? You can be sure that if you allow the Lord to set a watch over your tongue and let His Word dwell in you, then your words will be His gracious words.

OUR GRACIOUS SPIRIT

Do not grieve the Holy Spirit of God,
by whom you were sealed for the day of redemption.

EPHESIANS 4:30

The Holy Spirit grieves (is saddened) when believers don't exchange their old lifestyle for the new one. He is grieved when believers lie and obscure the truth, when they're angry and unforgiving, when they steal and refuse to share, and when they speak corruptly and lack a spirit of graciousness.

When you were saved, the Spirit of God put a seal on you, declaring that you belong to God forever. Since He has been gracious enough to give you eternal salvation, seal you forever, and keep your salvation secure until the day of redemption, how could you willfully grieve Him? He has done so much for you that, as a token of gratitude, you should not grieve Him.

A VIEW OF FORGIVENESS

Be kind to one another, tenderhearted,
forgiving one another,
even as God in Christ forgave you.

EPHESIANS 4:32

God was kind and tenderhearted toward you, forgiving you even when you didn't deserve it. If you base your attitude toward people on what they deserve, you've missed the point. Don't yell at people, slander them, or get angry with them, even if they deserve it. Those who exemplify God's character are loving, kind, tender, and forgiving. That's the kind of attitude God expects from those who are His new creations in Christ.

LIVING OUR MESSAGE

Whatever you do in word or deed,
do all in the name of the Lord Jesus,
giving thanks to God the Father through Him.

COLOSSIANS 3:17

Unbelievers might pay more attention to our gospel message if we gave them something special to notice. We could start by not lying and always speaking the truth. What if we never became angry in a sinful way but always acted in love; never stole but always shared; and never spoke in a coarse manner but always spoke edifying words? Can you imagine how the lost might react if we never were bitter, wrathful, resentful, violent, or slanderous but were always characterized by kindness, tenderheartedness, and forgiveness? Perhaps they would pay more attention then.

Examine your own actions. Do you speak the truth? Do you have control over your anger so that it operates only in righteousness? Do you share your resources with others? Do you speak graciously? Are you kind, tenderhearted, and forgiving? If you are a new man or woman in Christ, you will live like that.

GOD'S STANDARD

You shall therefore be holy,
for I am holy.

LEVITICUS 11:45

 The Christian life could be summed up in this one statement: be mimics, or imitators, of God. Jesus said, "Therefore you shall be perfect, just as your Father in heaven is perfect" (Matt. 5:48). The apostle Peter reiterated that high standard when he said, "But as He who called you is holy, you also be holy in all your conduct, because it is written, 'Be holy, for I am holy.'"

The more you know God, the more you'll understand who He wants you to be, so the primary pursuit of any believer is to know God (Phil. 3:10). That can be achieved only when we study God's character as it is revealed in Scripture.

Be a Mimic

Be imitators of God as dear children.

Ephesians 5:1

Imitating God may be easy to discuss, but it is difficult to do. You cannot do it in your own strength. But Jesus gave us the starting point for imitating God in the Sermon on the Mount. We need to mourn over our sin with a broken and contrite spirit. When we are overwhelmed by our sinfulness, we will hunger and thirst for righteousness. So there is a paradox: we are to be like God, yet we must know we cannot be like Him on our own.

Once we are aware of the paradox, then we know there must be some other power to make imitating God a possibility. The apostle Paul prayed that God would strengthen us "with might through His Spirit in the inner man" (Eph. 3:16). The Holy Spirit provides the strength "that you may be filled with all the fullness of God" (v. 19). We can be like God (in terms of His character), but we can't do it on our own—that is the Spirit's work.

MEASURE YOUR LOVE

God, who is rich in mercy, because of
His great love with which He loved us.

EPHESIANS 2:4

The greatest measuring rod of love in the life of a Christian may be forgiveness. That's because God showed His love to us in terms of forgiveness. The Bible could have taught us that God so loved the world that He made pretty flowers or trees or mountains. But it teaches that "God so loved the world that He gave His only begotten Son, that whoever believes in Him should not perish but have everlasting life" (John 3:16). He gave His Son to forgive us. That certainly shows God's love more than flowers, trees, or mountains.

Measure your love. Ask yourself, *Do I love?* If you don't, you are not one of God's own because the children of God love others (1 John 4:7–8). How can you know whether you are characterized by love? Ask yourself, *Am I bitter toward someone because of something he did to me? Do I often get angry with people, either externally or internally? Do I speak maliciously behind people's backs?* Those are characteristics of your old lifestyle—characteristics you must get rid of in order to love and forgive others.

THE DEPTH OF LOVE

Above all things have fervent love for one another,
for "love will cover a multitude of sins."

1 PETER 4:8

Christians are to love to the limit, which involves covering a "multitude of sins." Sin must be dealt with but must also be forgiven. That's what "cover" implies. We are to put a blanket over past sin that has been dealt with.

Examine yourself. Do you hold a grudge against someone in your house? If you do, remember that Jesus already paid the penalty for whatever that person did wrong. Your inability to forgive belies your love. And if a lack of forgiveness is characteristic of your life, you may not be a Christian.

Inevitably, those who have the greatest sense of forgiveness are quickest to forgive others. The people who know they've been forgiven much are able to forgive much. I hope that's true of you.

UNCONDITIONAL LOVE

*Christ also has loved us and given
Himself for us, an offering and a sacrifice
to God for a sweet-smelling aroma.*

EPHESIANS 5:2

The Bible doesn't refer to Christian love as an emotion but as an act of self-sacrifice. A person who truly loves someone else doesn't try to get anything out of that person. That's because godly love is never conditioned on a response—it is unconditional.

The world often defines love in terms of what it can get. But God loves even if He never gets anything in return. If that kind of love characterized our marriages, the divorce rate wouldn't be what it is today. If those who claim they don't love their spouses anymore would commit themselves to loving them unconditionally, they just might find that they can recapture or rebuild their love. Our Lord Jesus Christ doesn't love us for what He can get out of us; He loves us in spite of the hurt we cause Him. Make unconditional love your goal, and be humble, obedient, and self-sacrificing.

THE WORLD'S
SEARCH FOR LOVE

Above all these things put on love,
which is the bond of perfection.

COLOSSIANS 3:14

The people of the world want love very much. Loving, being loved, and making love are viewed as the ultimate high. Love is seen as the way to experience emotional extremes: you'll never be as happy nor as sad as when you're in love.

Today's music feeds that quest for love. Throughout much of it is the same underlying message: either the fantasy of a love sought or the despair of a love lost. People continue to chase that elusive dream. They base their concept of love on what it does for them. Songs, plays, films, books, and TV programs continually perpetuate the fantasy—the dream of a perfect love perfectly fulfilled.

The world's love is unforgiving, conditional, and self-centered. It focuses on desire, self-pleasure, and lust—the very opposite of God's perfect love. People search for love, but it's not true love; it is Satan's perversion.

SATAN'S BILL OF GOODS

But fornication and all uncleanness or covetousness,
let it not even be named among you, as is fitting for saints;
neither filthiness, nor foolish talking, nor coarse jesting,
which are not fitting, but rather giving of thanks.

EPHESIANS 5:3–4

God's love and the love of His children is forgiving, unconditional, and self-sacrificing, but you can be sure Satan will pervert that. Worldly love is shallow, selfish, sensual, and sexual, and Satan has sold that definition of love to the world.

In contrast to the world's love, today's verse concludes by indicating that we are to give thanks. Paul said, "In everything give thanks; for this is the will of God in Christ Jesus for you" (1 Thess. 5:18). When we are thankful for everything, we step outside ourselves, because thanksgiving is directed toward God.

Instead of taking from people, love them in a way that communicates thankfulness. Remember, God's love is unselfish and thankful, but the world's love is selfish and thankless.

AVOID THE CAVE

Walk while you have the light, lest darkness overtake you;
he who walks in darkness does not know where he is going.

JOHN 12:35

 When a Christian sins and engages in the deeds of darkness, it's as if he has had a relapse.

Imagine yourself lost in a cave. As you attempt to find your way out, you only proceed deeper and deeper into the network of tunnels. Soon you're in the belly of the earth. You're scared. Your heart is pounding. Your eyes are wide open, but all you can see is an oppressive blackness. You grope for hours, and the hours become a day, and then another day. All hope seems lost. Suddenly, off in the distance, there is a pinpoint of light. You move toward it, groping lest you fall into a deeper pit. Finally the light begins to widen and you find yourself at an opening in the cave! With your remaining strength you charge out into the daylight. You then know a freedom like nothing you had ever conceived was possible. However, not long after your escape you decide there were several things you enjoyed in the cave. So you go back in. How foolish! Yet that is essentially what a Christian does when he follows after deeds of darkness.

THE PROOF'S IN THE LIGHT

Finding out what is acceptable to the Lord.

EPHESIANS 5:10

The joy of a Christian is to be a living example of God's truth—to be a living verification of what is pleasing to Him.

When I was in Damascus, I discovered that the shops don't have windows. If you want to buy something, you have to take it out into the street and hold it up to the light to detect any flaws. Similarly, the only way to evaluate our lives is to expose every action, decision, and motive to the light of Christ and His Word.

When I go to the airport and put my suitcase through the scanner, I never worry about what the guard might see. I don't have anything to hide. I don't carry any guns or bombs. That's the way we ought to be as Christians. We shouldn't mind having the light reveal what we are, because it should only verify the truthfulness of our identity. We ought to be willing to expose our lives to light so that it will prove that we are light.

Exposing Sin

Have no fellowship with the unfruitful
works of darkness, but rather expose them.

Ephesians 5:11

Rather than doing what people in the world do, we ought to be exposing their evil. You could call us the spiritual CIA: our job is to expose the crimes of darkness. Our tool is the Word of God: "All Scripture is inspired by God and profitable for teaching, for *reproof,* for correction, for training in righteousness" (2 Tim. 3:16, NASB; emphasis added). Our life and our words should expose evil.

Sometimes just the way you live can expose the evil in people's lives. Have you ever walked up to people who know you're a Christian and who happen to be in the middle of a filthy conversation? Does it suddenly turn clean? When some unbelievers I happened to be playing golf with found out I was a pastor, their words and attitudes changed immediately.

We also are commissioned by God to verbally expose the evil of the world. We must diagnose it, confront it, and then offer the solution. Sin is a cancer that must be removed. You aren't helping anyone by ignoring it. People need to be convicted about their sin before they will ever see their need for a Savior.

WAKE UP!

Therefore He says, "Awake, you who sleep,
arise from the dead, and Christ will give you light."

EPHESIANS 5:14

Today's verse quotes what the prophet Isaiah said in Isaiah 60:1: "Arise, shine, for your light has come! And the glory of the Lord is risen upon you." That verse looked forward to the Messiah, and Paul's interpretation looks back to what Christ has done.

Many Bible commentators believe that Ephesians 5:14 is a line from an Easter hymn sung by the early church. They see it as an invitation—a gospel presentation. The sinner is the one who sleeps, and the invitation is to awake and arise. The Savior is Christ, who will give light.

Like Rip Van Winkle, men and women are sleeping through an age—an age of grace. When they wake up it will be too late. So Paul encourages them, as should we, to awake and arise from the dead.

Practice

July

JULY 1

THE VALUE
OF SELF-DISCIPLINE

Therefore I run thus: not with uncertainty.
1 CORINTHIANS 9:26

Today's culture is obsessed with entertainment, sports, materialism, and emotional gratification. In fact, those excessive preoccupations have become the marks of our shallow, amoral, and often immoral society.

A century ago President Theodore Roosevelt essentially predicted those results when he said that prosperity at any price, peace at any price, safety first instead of duty first, the love of soft living, and the get-rich theory of life would eventually destroy America.

One sure antidote to such a lifestyle is the self-discipline evidenced in the genuine Christian life. Your spiritual guidance and power come from the Lord, but you need self-discipline if He is to work effectively through you.

Paul wrote to Timothy, "For bodily exercise profits a little, but godliness is profitable for all things, having promise of the life that now is and of that which is to come" (1 Tim. 4:8). Ask God to make that true for you.

WHY BE SELF-DISCIPLINED?

*Be diligent to present
yourself approved to God.*

2 TIMOTHY 2:15

Concerning disciplined living, Richard Shelley Taylor writes, "Disciplined character belongs to the person who achieves balance by bringing all his faculties and powers under control. . . . He resolutely faces his duty. He is governed by a sense of responsibility. He has inward resources and personal reserves which are the wonder of weaker souls. He brings adversity under tribute, and compels it to serve him."

The Lord uses only the disciplined mind to think clearly, understand His Word, and present its truth effectively to the world. Only the disciplined mind consistently discerns truth from error. And only the disciplined Christian is a good testimony, within the church and before the world.

Simply stated, self-discipline is obedience to God's Word and willingness to submit everything in life to His will, for His ultimate glory.

Being Self-disciplined

*To this end I also labor, striving according
to His working which works in me mightily.*

Colossians 1:29

As a Christian, learn to cultivate self-discipline. Here are some practical ways to reach that objective:

Start small. In your home, for example, begin the housekeeping in the main bedroom. When that discipline is established, extend it to the rest of your home.

Be punctual. Make it a habit to be on time.

Deal with difficult tasks first. If you do the hardest jobs first, you will not leave them undone.

Be organized. Instead of merely reacting to circumstances, plan your day and your week.

Be grateful for correction. Don't shun constructive criticism; welcome it as a means for self-improvement.

Practice self-denial. This can begin in simple ways—substitute a healthy snack for junk food. Discipline in the physical realm carries over to the spiritual realm.

Take on responsibilities. Welcoming a new opportunity forces you to be organized.

These may seem insignificant, but they can be good practice in becoming a better servant of Christ.

AN ACCOUNTABLE LIFE

Therefore we make it our aim . . .
to be well pleasing to Him.

2 CORINTHIANS 5:9

It is unthinkable to believe that you can live a faithful, fruitful Christian life merely on good intentions and warm feelings. The Christian life is an accountable life, based on specific principles and standards. It is founded on divinely revealed values and beliefs to which God holds each of us.

A young man once asked me, "How can you know if you are truly a Christian? How can you know if your decision for Christ wasn't just an emotional experience?" I replied, "The only way to know if we have experienced justification, if we have been made right with Him and brought into His family, is by looking at our hearts and our lives. If Christ is our Savior and Lord, the deepest desire of our hearts will be to serve and to please Him, and that desire will be expressed in a longing for holiness and a pattern of righteous living."

A SUPERNATURAL LIFE

For it is God who works in you
both to will and to do for His good pleasure.

PHILIPPIANS 2:13

The obedient, productive Christian life is directed and empowered by the Holy Spirit. Therefore it is a supernatural life. It is foreign to the unregenerate person's thinking, and he can't attain such a life.

Supernatural living is conforming your outer life to your inner life, and living out the new nature you have in Jesus Christ. But it is not a mystical, undefined life based on abstract philosophical concepts. It is practical living derived from conscious obedience to God's commands. It is thinking, speaking, and acting in daily conformity to His Word and will.

THE GREATEST VIRTUE

He who abides in love abides in God,
and God in him.

1 JOHN 4:16

The greatest virtue of the Christian life is love. The New Testament proclaims agape love as the supreme virtue under which all others must line up. It centers on the needs and welfare of the one loved and pays the price necessary to meet those needs and foster that welfare.

Jesus clearly stated that the Bible's two greatest commandments are: "'You shall love the LORD your God with all your heart, with all your soul, and with all your mind.' And the second is like it: 'You shall love your neighbor as yourself'" (Matt. 22: 37–39).

Is this greatest of all scriptural virtues in your life?

The Most Important Gift

And now abide faith, hope, love,
these three; but the greatest of these is love.

1 Corinthians 13:13

If you're a Christian, love is more important than any spiritual gift you may have. It is therefore not surprising that Scripture says that the first "fruit of the Spirit is love" (Gal. 5:22). And it makes sense that by our love for other Christians "'all will know that you are My disciples'" (John 13:35).

Genuine love is so integral to the Christian life that if you claim to follow Jesus, you must demonstrate such love in order for your profession of faith to be valid (1 John 3:14).

BELIEVERS HATE EVIL

Hate what is evil.

ROMANS 12:9, NIV

 Evil is the antithesis of holiness and therefore the antithesis of godliness. So the child of God hates evil because God hates evil (paraphrase of Prov. 8:13).

If you truly love God you will fervently hate every form of evil. Because he loved God so much, David resolved that "a perverse heart shall depart from me; I will know no evil" (Ps. 101:4, NASB). The faithful Christian should never compromise with evil.

REFUSING TO BE ENTICED

Abstain from every form of evil.

1 THESSALONIANS 5:22

Hatred of evil leads to avoidance of it. You can't dabble with sin and avoid falling into it. Refusing to be enticed by temptation, the righteous person's "delight is in the law of the Lord, and in His law he meditates day and night" (Ps. 1:2).

You can't pursue righteousness and at the same time tolerate evil. That's why Paul counseled Timothy and all believers with this message: "Flee also youthful lusts; but pursue righteousness, faith, love, peace with those who call on the Lord out of a pure heart" (2 Tim. 2:22).

HOLDING ON
TO WHAT'S GOOD

Cling to what is good.

ROMANS 12:9

As a servant of Jesus Christ, God wants you to bind yourself to everything good, to whatever is inherently right and worthy. That task requires the use of discernment. With the help of God and His Word, you must carefully evaluate everything and thoughtfully decide what to reject and what to cling to (1 Thess. 5:21–22).

As you separate yourself from worldly things and saturate yourself with Scripture, that which is good will increasingly replace that which is evil. Then, you will fulfill Paul's message to the Romans: "Do not be conformed to this world, but be transformed by the renewing of your mind, that you may prove what is that good and acceptable and perfect will of God" (12:2).

Brotherly Love

*Be kindly affectionate
to one another with brotherly love.*

Romans 12:10

Brotherly love reflects the nature of Christians. That's why Paul doesn't hesitate to remind believers to practice that virtue, "Concerning brotherly love you have no need that I should write to you, for you yourselves are taught by God to love one another" (1 Thess. 4:9).

The true disciple of Jesus knows intuitively he should love his brothers and sisters in Christ. Because they have the same heavenly Father, love among believers is as normal as the affection between members of a family. If you are a true disciple, such love will be true of you.

HONORING ONE ANOTHER

*In honor giving
preference to one another.*

ROMANS 12:10

If you are devoted to brotherly love, it goes without saying that you'll give preference to other believers. That means you'll have genuine humility and will not "think of [yourself] more highly than [you] ought to think" (Rom. 12:3; see also Phil. 2:3). It also means you will give honor to fellow Christians and take the initiative to put them first.

You will not flatter another believer merely in the hope of having the compliment returned or to gain favor with them. Instead, you'll express to them real appreciation, respect, and love as a fellow member of the family of God.

SHOWING DILIGENCE

Not lagging in diligence.

ROMANS 12:11

Diligence applies to whatever you do in your Christian life. Anything done in the Lord's service is worth doing with enthusiasm and care.

Jesus knew His time of earthly ministry was limited and that He needed to make the most of every opportunity to serve His heavenly Father. We also "must work . . . while it is day; the night is coming when no one can work" (John 9:4). And other Christians will certainly appreciate our diligent good works, as Paul urged, "Let us do good to all, especially to those who are of the household of faith" (Gal. 6:10).

No Room for Lethargy

Whatever your hand finds to do,
do it with all your might.

ECCLESIASTES 9:10, NASB

There's no room for lethargy in the Christian life. Such a posture not only prevents you from doing good, but it sometimes means that you've actually allowed evil to prosper. For weeds to flourish, the gardener need only leave the garden alone.

The author of Hebrews alluded to the reward God has for those who serve Him diligently, "For God is not unjust to forget your work and labor of love which you have shown toward His name, in that you have ministered to the saints, and do minister" (Heb. 6:10).

THE ENTHUSIASTIC ATTITUDE

Fervent in spirit.

ROMANS 12:11

One of humanity's most chronic shortcomings is the lack of individual enthusiasm. Often our failures to achieve what we ought result directly from apathy and lack of commitment. But that should not be true if you're a Christian.

Enthusiasm requires Spirit-assisted resolve and persistence, not just human-guided good intentions. Henry Martyn, the tireless missionary to India, conducted his ministry with scriptural enthusiasm and fervency. It was his desire to "burn out for God." And the apostle Paul admonishes us to "not grow weary while doing good, for in due season we shall reap if we do not lose heart" (Gal. 6:9).

TRUE SERVICE

Serving the Lord.

ROMANS 12:11

Everything you do in the Christian life should be consistent with God's Word and truly in His service and to His glory. In Romans 12:11, the word Paul used to describe Christian service refers to the service of a bond-slave, whose sole duty was to carry out his master's will. That is how you ought to serve God—as a bond servant of Jesus Christ.

But you can't serve the Lord in your own power any more than you could come to Him by your own power or will. The power to serve Christ comes from God. "To this end I also labor," Paul testified, "striving according to His working which works in me mightily" (Col. 1:29).

GENUINE PRAYER

Continuing steadfastly in prayer.

ROMANS 12:12

For dedicated Christians, steadfast prayer will be as continual in their spiritual life as breathing is in their physical life. That was true of early believers and how they worshiped, both before and after the arrival of the Holy Spirit at Pentecost (Acts 1:14; 2:42). The church first appointed deacons so the apostles could devote themselves "continually to prayer and to the ministry of the word" (Acts 6:4).

God wants you to pray "with the spirit, and . . . with the understanding" (1 Cor. 14:15) and "without ceasing" (1 Thess. 5:17). That's why Paul encouraged Timothy to have "the men pray everywhere, lifting up holy hands" (1 Tim. 2:8).

THE SPIRIT OF SHARING

*Share with God's people
who are in need.*

ROMANS 12:13, NIV

Society says we each have a claim on certain possessions, but God says we own nothing. You are simply a steward of whatever He has blessed you with. And part of that stewardship responsibility is to occasionally share your personal resources with fellow Christians who have needs.

The spirit of sharing was immediately evident in the early church as believers after Pentecost "continued steadfastly in the apostles' doctrine and fellowship, in the breaking of bread, and in prayers. . . . [and] all who believed were together, and had all things in common" (Acts 2:42, 44; see also 1 Tim. 6:17–18). Ask the Lord to help you demonstrate that same spirit of sharing.

BIBLICAL HOSPITALITY

Given to hospitality.

ROMANS 12:13

True followers of Christ should not only meet the needs of believers and unbelievers whom they encounter, but they should also look for opportunities to help those they don't know. That is the scriptural definition of hospitality. Hebrews 13:2 instructs us, "Do not forget to entertain strangers, for by so doing some have unwittingly entertained angels."

You should view any opportunity to demonstrate hospitality as a happy privilege, not a drudging duty (1 Pet. 4:9). Gaius undoubtedly had that sort of righteous attitude in his hospitality toward itinerant teachers, because the apostle John commended him: "Beloved, you do faithfully whatever you do for the brethren and for strangers, who have borne witness of your love before the church. If you send them forward on their journey in a manner worthy of God, you will do well" (3 John 5–6).

LOVE YOUR ENEMIES

Bless those who persecute you;
bless and do not curse.

ROMANS 12:14

The Bible commands us not only to resist hating and retaliating against those who might harm us, but it tells us to go beyond that and actually bless them. That's what Jesus instructed to those who heard His Sermon on the Mount: " 'But I say to you who hear: Love your enemies, do good to those who hate you, bless those who curse you, and pray for those who spitefully use you' " (Luke 6:27–28).

To truly love your enemies, you must treat them as if they were your friends.

SHARING OTHERS' JOY

Rejoice with those who rejoice.

ROMANS 12:15

At first glance, the concept of sharing someone else's joy seems easy enough to accept. But when that person's blessings, honor, and welfare come at your expense or perhaps make your circumstances appear unsatisfying by comparison, you naturally want to be resentful or jealous rather than happy.

However, it is distinctively Christian for you to rejoice in the good circumstances and rewards of others—especially other Christians—no matter what your own situation might be. "If one member is honored, all the members rejoice with it" (1 Cor. 12:26).

SHARING OTHERS' SORROW

Weep with those who weep.

ROMANS 12:15

God wants you to be sensitive to the sorrows and difficulties of others. That's compassion, which by definition goes even beyond the duty of empathizing and sympathizing with someone. It means to actually enter into the suffering of others.

God is a compassionate God (Deut. 4:31), so much so that Scripture declares "His compassions fail not. They are new every morning" (Lam. 3:22–23). The Son of God was genuinely compassionate, displaying the tenderheartedness of the Father as He wept with Mary and Martha at the grave of their brother Lazarus (John 11:35).

If you are a child of God, how can you do any less than reflect your Lord's compassionate character? "Therefore, as God's chosen people, holy and dearly loved, clothe yourselves with compassion, kindness, humility, gentleness and patience" (Col. 3:12, NIV).

NO FAVORITISM ALLOWED

For there is no partiality with God.

ROMANS 2:11

It is a sin for a Christian to show favoritism to people. That is, he should not be prejudiced for or against another person simply based on position, wealth, influence, popularity, or appearance.

The clearest, most practical New Testament teaching on impartiality is in James' letter to believers:

> My brethren, do not hold the faith of our Lord Jesus Christ, the Lord of glory, with partiality. For if there should come into your assembly a man with gold rings, in fine apparel, and there should also come in a poor man in filthy clothes, and you pay attention to the one wearing the fine clothes . . . have you not shown partiality among yourselves, and become judges with evil thoughts? . . . but if you show partiality, you commit sin, and are convicted by the law as transgressors (2:1–4, 9).

If God never plays favorites, shouldn't you strive for the same virtuous character, "doing nothing with partiality" (1 Tim. 5:21)?

HAVING A HEART
FOR THE LOWLY

*Do not be proud, but be willing to
associate with people of low position.*

ROMANS 12:16, NIV

There is no aristocracy in the church, no place for an ecclesiastical elite that deserves all the attention. But the Bible doesn't say you should never associate with wealthy or influential people. It's simply that you should sense more of an obligation to serve the lowly people because they are the more needy.

The Lord Jesus fittingly illustrated this truth, "'When you give a dinner or a supper, do not ask your friends, your brothers, your relatives, nor rich neighbors, lest they also invite you back, and you be repaid. But when you give a feast, invite the poor, the maimed, the lame, the blind. And you will be blessed, because they cannot repay you; for you shall be repaid at the resurrection of the just'" (Luke 14:12–14).

It's not wrong to invite friends and relatives to your home for a meal. But it is wrong to do so with selfish motives, with the notion of being rewarded, and with no regard for those who can't repay you.

HUMILITY SHOULD RULE

Do not be conceited.

ROMANS 12:16, NIV

Conceited, self-serving Christians are a serious contradiction. If we would follow Christ we must be submissive to God's will as contained in His Word. Any confidence you have in yourself, your own wisdom, or your natural talents must be subordinated to the Lord's commands.

In no way should you be conceited, or in any respect consider yourself better than fellow believers. Instead, God wants you to accept and embrace every member of the body of Christ: "Let each of you look out not only for his own interests, but also for the interests of others" (Phil. 2:4).

No Such Thing as Payback

Repay no one evil for evil.

ROMANS 12:17

Some people believe the Old Testament law of "eye for eye, tooth for tooth" (Exod. 21:24) permits personal revenge. But that's not what it refers to. It was actually saying that the severity of legal punishment should not exceed the severity of an offense. In other words, if someone put out another person's eye, he could not be penalized by anything involving more than the forfeiture of his own eye.

The authority to avenge civil and criminal injustices belongs by divine mandate only to governments. God forbids us from exacting personal vengeance. The apostle Peter summarized the principle this way: "Finally, all of you be of one mind . . . not returning evil for evil or reviling for reviling, but on the contrary blessing, knowing that you were called to this, that you may inherit a blessing" (1 Pet. 3:8–9).

RESPECTING
WHAT IS RIGHT

Respect what is right in the sight of all men.

ROMANS 12:17, NASB

If you sincerely respect others, including your enemies, you will be predisposed to do the right thing concerning them. Such respect helps you to discipline and prepare yourself ahead of time to respond in all situations in a manner pleasing to God.

Behaving in a way that respects what is right and demonstrates graciousness and forgiveness toward others, even your enemies, should be a positive testimony to them. It will also "adorn the doctrine of God our Savior in all things" (Titus 2:10).

PEACEFUL
RELATIONSHIPS

Live peaceably with all men.

ROMANS 12:18

By definition, a peaceful relationship cannot be one-sided. You must do your part to make sure that your side of a relationship is right. Your inner desire, with God's help, should be to live in peace with everyone, even the most sinful, hard-to-get-along-with people.

Short of compromising the Word of God, you ought to extend yourself to great lengths to build peaceful bridges to those who persecute you and hate you. If you set aside any grudge or bitterness and from the heart completely forgive your enemies, you can honestly seek reconciliation with them.

OVERCOMING EVIL WITH GOOD

Do not be overcome by evil, but overcome evil with good.

ROMANS 12:21

Returning good for evil is one of the most difficult obligations a Christian has. Yet from Old Testament times, that has been God's command to the godly person: "If your enemy is hungry, give him bread to eat; and if he is thirsty, give him water to drink; for so you will heap coals of fire on his head, and the Lord will reward you" (Prov. 25:21–22).

The expression "heap coals of fire on his head" referred to an ancient Egyptian custom. A person wanting to show public contrition would carry on his head a pan of burning coals to symbolize the burning pain of his shame and guilt. When you love an enemy enough to truly endeavor to meet his needs, you hope to shame him for his hatred toward you.

To avoid being overcome by the evil done to you, you must first not allow it to overwhelm you. Second, you must not allow your own evil responses to overpower you. In either instance, the evil itself must be overcome by what is good.

WHO IS YOUR NEIGHBOR?

You shall love your neighbor as yourself.

MATTHEW 22:39

Jesus answered the Jewish lawyer's question, "Who is my neighbor?" with the parable of the Good Samaritan (Luke 10:30–37). In this familiar story, a Jewish man is beaten and left for dead on the road. A compassionate Samaritan rescues the man, even though Samaritans and Jews normally hated one another.

The point of the story is that your neighbor is whoever comes across your path with a need. Would you have reacted the way the Samaritan did if you had encountered the injured man along the side of the road? Hopefully you would not have passed him by, as the priest and Levite did in the story.

The lesson of the parable is not that you must stop and help everyone who has a flat tire, or that you have to give money to every panhandler you meet. But God wants you to be sensitive to such situations and willing to help if you think your assistance is the only aid the person is likely to receive. In other words, follow the Golden Rule: "'Therefore, whatever you want men to do to you, do also to them'" (Matt. 7:12).

REPROGRAMMED
FOR RIGHTEOUSNESS

Your word I have hidden in my heart,
that I might not sin against You.

PSALM 119:11

A man once said to me, "I've come to Christ, but I still have so much garbage in my mind. How do I clean it out?" I answered him, "You've been programmed by the world for a long time, so your mind is full of filth. Therefore, it has to be reprogrammed—completely cleansed."

The only way to reprogram your mind with God's righteousness is to read, study, and meditate on the Word of God. "Let the word of Christ dwell in you richly in all wisdom, teaching and admonishing one another in psalms and hymns and spiritual songs, singing with grace in your hearts to the Lord" (Col. 3:16).

If you're a Christian, and you submit to the Holy Spirit as you study Scripture, you will have a reprogrammed mind that focuses on God's righteousness and helps you live accordingly (Rom. 12:1–2; Phil. 4:8).

Crossroads

AUGUST

The Great Choice

Choose for yourselves
this day whom you will serve.

Joshua 24:15

The Sermon on the Mount presents us with the most crucial of spiritual choices. Its ethical truths bless those who believe and obey Christ but judge those who reject Him.

The spiritual choice, which you must not ignore or postpone, concerns the way of salvation. There is one true way to be right with God, and there are many false ways. It is wrong to say that *all* roads lead to heaven—only *one* does. You must reject all of the works-oriented ways people have devised to reach heaven and embrace the one way God Himself has provided—faith in His saving grace as displayed in the atoning death of His Son (Acts 4:12; 1 Tim. 2:5–6).

TWO RELIGIONS

*How long will you falter
between two opinions?*

1 KINGS 18:21

Humanity has always had two systems of religion available. One is from God and is based on His gracious accomplishment. The other is from mankind and is based on the achievements of men and women. One is all of sovereign grace and is embraced by faith. The other is all of human works and is performed in the flesh. One flows out of a sincere heart, the other from outward hypocrisy.

Even Moses' law, though from God, was not a means of salvation. It was a means of showing people their need for salvation. "Therefore by the deeds of the law no flesh will be justified in His sight, for by the law is the knowledge of sin" (Rom. 3:20). When Jesus came, He taught us that we are incapable in ourselves of keeping that perfect law. He made it clear that we must choose the religion of grace and faith rather than the religion of law and works.

The Narrow Gate

Enter by the narrow gate.

Matthew 7:13

Many people have admired the principles taught in the Sermon on the Mount, but most have not followed those principles. Many have respected Jesus as a great teacher but have never received Him as Savior and Lord. That's because they failed to enter "the narrow gate"—God's right gate, the only one that leads to eternal life.

The path to the narrow way of Christian living is through the narrow gate of Christ Himself. "'I am the way, the truth, and the life. No one comes to the Father except through Me'" (John 14:6). Have you gone through the narrow gate?

THE ONLY GOSPEL

Nor is there salvation in any other.

ACTS 4:12

If you testify to others that the gospel of Jesus Christ is the only gospel, the only way to God, you are not merely proclaiming your own view of right religion but God's revelation of truth. You do not proclaim the gospel of Christ simply because you know it, because it suits your personality, or because you want to be intolerant and exclusive. You declare the gospel of Christ because it's God's only way for people to find salvation from sin and eternal death.

You proclaim Jesus' gospel as the only gospel because He said, "'I am the door. If anyone enters by Me, he will be saved'" (John 10:9). You testify to this gospel because you agree with the apostle Paul that "there is one God and one Mediator between God and men, the Man Christ Jesus" (1 Tim. 2:5).

You're therefore in good company and on solid footing when you testify of God's *only* way of salvation to those who don't know Jesus Christ.

Entering the Gate

Not by works of righteousness which
we have done, but according to His mercy He saved us.

When you enter the narrow gate of salvation, you must do so alone. A turnstile perhaps best represents the concept of the narrow gate. Just one person at a time—with no baggage—can pass through a turnstile. God has ordained that people enter His kingdom singly, not in groups. You can't ride in on the coattails of your church, your family, or your friends, no matter how godly those people are.

God's gate is so narrow that you must go through it not only alone but naked. You can't go through the gate clothed in sin and self-will. As the hymn writer said, "Nothing in my hand I bring, simply to Thy cross I cling." That's the way of the cross, which is the gospel. And the gospel is the narrow gate, which involves self-denial. Jesus said, "'If anyone desires to come after Me, let him deny himself, and take up his cross, and follow Me. For whoever desires to save his life will lose it, but whoever loses his life for My sake will find it'" (Matt. 16:24–25).

THE RICH YOUNG RULER

*How hard it is for those who have
riches to enter the kingdom of God!*

LUKE 18:24

 When the rich young ruler approached Jesus concerning salvation, our Lord immediately tested his willingness to deny all and follow Him: "'Sell all that you have and distribute to the poor, and you will have treasure in heaven; and come, follow Me'" (Luke 18:22). When the young ruler did not heed Jesus' words, he revealed an unwillingness to submit to the lordship of Christ.

Anyone who would come to salvation must yield control of his life to the Savior. That means being willing either to give up everything to follow Him, or to be content with all He has given you, with the realization that He may sovereignly give you more as you serve Him.

Salvation is the exchange of all that you are for all that Christ is. Saving faith, therefore, is not merely an act of the mind; it counts the cost (Luke 14:28) and humbly cries out to God as did the publican in Luke 18:13, "'God, be merciful to me a sinner!'"

Are you counting the cost today and every day?

Childlike Dependency

Unless you are converted and become
as little children, you will by no means
enter the kingdom of heaven.

Matthew 18:3

When speaking of genuine salvation, Jesus made an apt comparison to the characteristics of young children. To be saved, you must come to Christ with the dependent attitude and outlook of a little child: simple, helpless, trusting, unaffected, unpretentious, and unambitious.

It's not that children are without sin, but that they are naïve and unassuming, dependent on others and free from selfish claims to grandeur. They submit to the care of their parents and other loved ones, relying on them to meet all their needs. That's the kind of humble and dependent attitude anyone must have who seeks to enter the kingdom of Jesus Christ.

REPENTANCE
NOT OPTIONAL

Repent, and believe in the gospel.

MARK 1:15

If you want to enter the narrow gate you must repent. Many Jews during Jesus' time believed that just being physical descendants of Abraham was sufficient for entrance into heaven. And many people today believe that simply being churchgoers or morally good people qualifies them for salvation. After all, they reason, God is too benevolent to exclude anyone but the most evil people.

God does desire that everyone enter the narrow gate because He is "not willing that any should perish but that all should come to repentance" (2 Pet. 3:9). But you will not pass through the narrow gate unless you follow Charles Spurgeon's admonition: "You and your sins must separate or you and your God will never come together. No one sin may you keep; they must all be given up, they must be brought out like Canaanite kings from the cave and be hanged up in the sun."

THE REPENTANT LIFE

Thus also faith by itself,
if it does not have works, is dead.

JAMES 2:17

If you have turned away from your sins and turned toward God's way of righteousness, you *will* live a changed life. The theme of 1 John is that the truly redeemed person will demonstrate a truly transformed life. "Whoever keeps His word, truly the love of God is perfected in him. By this we know that we are in Him. He who says he abides in Him ought himself also to walk just as He walked" (1 John 2:5–6).

Those who teach that repentance and the repentant lifestyle aren't a necessary part of the gospel are not presenting the gospel Jesus offered. Such a gospel of self-satisfaction and self-righteousness is from the world, not God.

THE NARROW WAY

The way is narrow that leads to life.

MATTHEW 7:14, NASB

The narrow gate to salvation leads to the correspondingly narrow way of righteous living. By contrast, the broad gate to condemnation leads to the broad way of careless, unrighteous living.

There was once a West Indian who chose Islam over Christianity because to him Islam "is a noble, broad path. There is room for a man and his sins on it. The way of Christ is too narrow." Sadly, too many professing Christians today don't see the issue as clearly as that unbelieving Muslim. They don't understand or accept Jesus' definition of the narrow way as the difficult, demanding way. It is the life of self-denial and intense effort. If you are living that life you will "fight the good fight of faith, lay hold on eternal life, to which you were also called" (1 Tim. 6:12).

AUGUST 11

THE BURDEN BEARER

My yoke is easy and My burden is light.

MATTHEW 11:30

Jesus described Himself as "'gentle and lowly in heart'" (Matt. 11:29); therefore, He gives rest, not weariness, to all those who submit to Him and do His work. In Christ you have not only a Savior but also a burden bearer. He helps you carry all your burdens, including the burden of obedience.

Jesus will never give you a burden too heavy to carry. His yoke has nothing to do with the demands of the law or human works. Instead, it pertains to the Christian's obedience to Him, which He wants to make a joyful and happy experience. Thank God for providing such a gracious burden bearer in the person of His Son.

DISCIPLESHIP IS SERIOUS

*For which of you, intending to build a tower,
does not sit down first and count the cost.*

LUKE 14:28

You can pay nothing to earn salvation; yet living for Christ is a serious matter of discipleship. To be a Christian means to rely on Christ's power rather than your own and to be willing to forsake your way for His. Being a Christian can mean facing persecution, ridicule, and tribulation. Jesus forewarned the disciples, "'If they persecuted Me, they will also persecute you'" (John 15:20).

But with His warning about the cost of discipleship, the Lord promised that your heart would rejoice "'and your joy no one will take from you'" (John 16:22). And He also told His followers to "'be of good cheer, I have overcome the world'" (16:33). You won't escape the difficulties of discipleship, but Jesus will enable you to handle them.

WISDOM FOR LIFE

Ask, and it will be given to you; seek, and you will find; knock, and it will be opened to you. For everyone who asks receives, and he who seeks finds, and to him who knocks it will be opened.

MATTHEW 7 : 7 – 8

To possess God's wisdom is among the greatest needs we have. God's wisdom helps us to make prudent choices throughout our Christian lives—to choose God's way and reject the world's way in every situation.

The Bible provides many commands and principles for godly living, but it is not an exhaustive manual of methods and rules for every conceivable situation. That would not be very workable. And it would keep us from relying directly on God. He wants us to be in His Word daily so that we can know His principles for righteous living and can pray wisely for guidance when we have difficult decisions.

In Scripture the Lord gives believers enough truth to live responsibly, but enough mystery to draw them to Him in believing prayer: "If any of you lacks wisdom, let him ask of God, who gives to all liberally and without reproach, and it will be given to him" (James 1:5).

THE RIGHT GROUP

There are few who find it.

MATTHEW 7:14

Those who are drawn by God's Spirit to enter at the narrow gate and travel the narrow way are in the right spiritual group. Those in the wrong spiritual group include all pagans and nominal Christians, all atheists and superficial religionists, all nominal theists and secular humanists, and people from all ethnic and economic backgrounds who don't have a saving faith in Jesus Christ. They enter through the wide gate and travel the broad way that leads to destruction.

Jesus said "'Many are called, but few are chosen'" (Matt. 22:14). The right group is not small simply because the gate is too narrow or the way is too restrictive. Believers are few because so many people refuse to repent of their sins and trust in Jesus for salvation. They would rather die in darkness (see John 3:19).

Everyone who wants to come to Jesus Christ can, with God's help, do so: "'All that the Father gives Me will come to Me, and the one who comes to Me I will by no means cast out'" (John 6:37). And those who come will forever be in the right group.

Beware of False Prophets

False christs and false prophets will
rise and show signs and wonders to deceive.

Mark 13:22

False prophets have been around since the beginning of redemptive history (see Deut. 13:1–5), and they always find a hearing. In His Olivet Discourse, Jesus warned, "'Take heed that no one deceives you. For many will come in My name . . . and will deceive many'" (Matt. 24:4–5). Years later the apostle John told his readers that "many deceivers have gone out into the world" (2 John 7).

False prophets have always enjoyed some degree of popularity because so many people do not want to hear the truth. Thus John admonished all believers, "Beloved, do not believe every spirit, but test the spirits, whether they are of God; because many false prophets have gone out into the world" (1 John 4:1).

WHAT IS A FALSE PROPHET?

You will know them by their fruits.

MATTHEW 7:16

 The most dangerous characteristic of false prophets is that they claim to be from God and to speak for Him. "The prophets prophesy falsely, and the priests rule by their own power; and My people love to have it so" (Jer. 5:31).

Such leaders nearly always appear pleasant and positive. They like to be with Christians, and they know how to talk and act like believers.

False prophets usually exude sincerity and thereby more easily deceive others (see 2 Tim. 3:13). But you can identify false teachers' true colors by noting what they do not talk much about. They usually *don't deny* basic doctrines such as Christ's deity and substitutionary atonement, the sinfulness of humanity, or unbelievers' going to hell. They simply *ignore* such "controversial" truths.

But whenever a false prophet is in your midst, you must not ignore his presence or the harmful effects of his heretical teaching.

RESPONDING
TO FALSE PROPHETS

Beware of false prophets, who come to you
in sheep's clothing, but inwardly they are ravenous wolves.
MATTHEW 7:15

In Jude's brief letter to believers, the apostle firmly warns against false prophets and tells us how to respond to them. "Keep yourselves in the love of God" (Jude 21). Our primary response to false teaching is simply to be right with God in the first place, to make sure we are in fellowship with Him and receiving His blessing and power. Then we can "have mercy on some, who are doubting" (v. 22, NASB)—believers who doubt their faith because of false teachers need reassurance.

Another necessary response might be to "save others, snatching them out of the fire" (v. 23, NASB)—unbelievers bound for hell after hearing false teaching need to be rescued before it's too late.

Finally, Jude tells about a third response to false prophets: "On some have mercy with fear, hating even the garment polluted by the flesh" (v. 23, NASB). We sometimes must confront false prophets and their followers, doing so with a special dependence on the Lord and being careful not to get contaminated by their false teachings.

DISCERNING
TRUE FROM FALSE

Every good tree bears good fruit,
but a bad tree bears bad fruit.

MATTHEW 7:17

The Didache, one of the earliest Christian writings after the New Testament, gives several guidelines for discerning true from false prophets. First, a true prophet will not wear out his welcome but will move on, tending to his ministry and mission. But a false prophet may hang around indefinitely, concerned only about serving his own interests.

Second, unlike the false prophet, the true prophet is averse to excessive appeals for money. He is content with support for the basic needs of life and ministry.

Third, a true prophet's lifestyle will correspond to the righteous standards he teaches. A false prophet very likely will teach one thing and practice another.

A true minister of the gospel will demonstrate what Paul wrote, "For we are not, as so many, peddling the word of God; but as of sincerity, but as from God, we speak in the sight of God in Christ" (2 Cor. 2:17).

JUDGING SPIRITUAL FRUIT

A good tree cannot bear bad fruit,
nor can a bad tree bear good fruit.

MATTHEW 7:18

A fruit tree may be beautiful and decorative and offer refreshing shade in the summer. But its main purpose is to bear fruit, and it is therefore judged by what it produces and not by how it appears. Similarly, anyone who claims to speak for God must be judged by his life, not merely by his appearance or words.

False prophets can sometimes deceive even genuine Christians. If you become careless concerning the Word of God, lazy about prayer, and apathetic about God's kingdom, it is easy for you to be deceived by a clever, pleasant, smooth-talking teacher who only appears to be orthodox.

Therefore it's crucial that you remain vigilant and well prepared. Bad fruit from a bad tree is simply not acceptable, no matter how good both may appear. It has to be examined carefully (see Heb. 5:14). But for the mature believer, there is true assurance in Jesus' words, "'by their fruits you will know them'" (Matt. 7:20). There is no need to be deceived if you look closely.

BEARING TRUE FRUIT

Bear fruits worthy of repentance.

LUKE 3:8

 Your essential character—your inner motives, convictions, loyalties, and ambitions—will eventually show through in what you say and do. Good works do not save you, but every believer is saved for good works. "For we are His workmanship, created in Christ Jesus for good works, which God prepared beforehand that we should walk in them" (Eph. 2:10; see also Gal. 5:22–23; Col. 1:10).

For the believer, true fruit-bearing occurs with the help of Christ. The apostle Paul speaks of our "being filled with the fruits of righteousness which are by Jesus Christ" (Phil. 1:11). On the other hand, unbelievers (including those who falsely profess Christ) will eventually demonstrate the bad fruit that their unregenerate lives inevitably produce.

If you are bearing fruit, you will be growing in all the areas Peter lists: faith, virtue, knowledge, self-control, perseverance, godliness, brotherly kindness, and love (see 2 Pet. 1:5–9).

Avoid False Creeds

The time will come when
they will not endure sound doctrine. . . .
But you be watchful in all things.

2 Timothy 4:3, 5

The prophet Isaiah gave this helpful counsel concerning recognizing false doctrine, "To the law and to the testimony! If they do not speak according to this word, it is because there is no light in them" (Isa. 8:20). Heretical doctrines and false creeds cannot withstand the scrutiny of Scripture's divine light.

False creeds never teach the necessity to enter through Christ's narrow gate or to walk on His narrow way. At first glance their contents may appear to be orthodox and to demand real faith, but ultimately their message will rest on the foundation of human works and will teach salvation by human effort. Such creeds will not reveal the depth or danger of sin and human depravity, and consequently will not advocate the need for repentance, forgiveness, and submission to the Lord.

The message of all false creeds is a message of gaps, the greatest of which omits the truth of the gospel that saves.

FALSE ASSURANCE

Not everyone who says to Me,
"Lord, Lord," shall enter the kingdom of heaven,
but he who does the will of My Father in heaven.

MATTHEW 7:21

The New Testament gives very high standards for discerning the true Christian life, and it also issues many warnings to avoid self-deception concerning salvation (see Matt. 25).

One of the causes of self-deception is a wrong understanding of the doctrine of assurance. Many people become self-deceived by well-meaning Christian witnesses who tell them that to be saved, they simply have to make a decision for Christ and then, based on that prayer of decision, never doubt their salvation again.

Sadly, such evangelistic workers are attempting to certify someone's salvation apart from the convicting work of the Holy Spirit and the future evidence of spiritual fruit accompanied by obedience to the Word (John 8:31). Only God can give a person real assurance of salvation, by the Spirit working through His Word (see Rom. 8:14–16).

Spiritual Self-examination

Test yourselves.

2 Corinthians 13:5

Many professed believers go through life with an indifferent attitude toward their sins. Yet the Lord tells His people to examine their lives each time they come to His table (1 Cor. 11:28). And the apostle Paul admonished the Corinthian church, "Examine yourselves as to whether you are in the faith. Test yourselves" (2 Cor. 13:5). If you do this regularly and with a positive attitude, you will make sure your inner motives and desires are set toward pleasing God, even though you often fail Him (see Rom. 7:14–25).

AVOIDING DECEPTION

Many will say to Me in that day, "Lord, Lord, have we not prophesied in Your name, cast out demons in Your name, and done many wonders in Your name?"

MATTHEW 7:22

A good way to avoid spiritual self-deception is simply to know and shun the types of religious pitfalls people can drop into. First, there is inordinate preoccupation with mere religious activities. The external focus on attending church services and Bible studies, listening to sermons, singing hymns, and other inherently good activities can actually insulate you from knowing the God you think you are serving.

Second, there is superficial reliance on past religious activities and ceremonies. Just because you were baptized as a child, attended Sunday school or vacation Bible school, or joined a church does not necessarily mean you are now right with God.

Third, there is a religious knowledge for its own sake. You may be commmitted to a certain denomination and its traditions or have an intense academic interest in theology. But these things are useless if you are not also interested in becoming more like Christ and more obedient to His Word.

FALSE VERSUS TRUE PROFESSION

What does it profit, my brethren,
if someone says he has faith but does not have works?

JAMES 2:14

A good tree not only can but also *will* bear good fruit. However, anyone who professes to be a good tree (a Christian) but does not bear the fruit of good works has no part in the body of Jesus Christ. The person who truly professes to be a Christian will be able to echo James' sentiments, "Faith by itself, if it does not have works, is dead. . . . Show me your faith without your works, and I will show you my faith by my works" (James 2:17–18).

THE SOLID FOUNDATION

*Therefore whoever hears these sayings of Mine,
and does them, I will liken him to a wise man
who built his house on the rock.*

MATTHEW 7:24

The wise person will build his life on the rock. The rock that Jesus is referring to in today's verse is God's Word, the Bible. Building on the rock is therefore equivalent to hearing and obeying Christ's words, and for us that means living according to Scripture.

After Peter confessed, "'You are the Christ, the Son of the living God,'" our Lord told him, "'. . . flesh and blood has not revealed this to you, but My Father who is in heaven. And I also say to you that you are Peter, and on this rock I will build My church'" (Matt. 16:16–18). Jesus' word for "rock" in this verse is the same one He used in Matthew 7:24. It is the bedrock of God's revelation, His Word. The rock of the solid foundation is the kind of sure, divine guidance Peter received, and it is the only base on which the true Christian life can rest.

THE HOUSE
BUILT ON THE ROCK

It did not fall,
for it was founded on the rock.

MATTHEW 7:25

The house founded on the rock represents the life of spiritual obedience. It's the life that takes a scriptural view of itself and the world, as described in Christ's Beatitudes in The Sermon on the Mount. It's the sort of life that's more concerned about internal righteousness than external form. It's a life of genuineness rather than hypocrisy, and of God's righteousness rather than self-righteousness.

The house based on the rock depicts the life that empties itself of pride and human good works and is humble and repentant because of its own sin. Such a life strives, with the Spirit's help, to enter the narrow gate of salvation and be faithful to the narrow way of Christ and His Word. The life built on the rock trusts in God's will and hopes in His Word above all else. Where does your hope rest and your trust lie?

The House on the Sand

*Everyone who hears these sayings of Mine,
and does not do them, will be like a foolish man
who built his house on the sand.*

Matthew 7:26

The house built on the sand symbolizes a spiritual life built on the foundation of human opinions, attitudes, and wills, which are always shifting and unstable. If you build your life on this foundation, you are building it on self-will, self-sufficiency, self-righteousness, self-purpose, and self-fulfillment. If you choose sandy foundations, your life will be based on false teaching and will fall short of salvation—"always learning and never able to come to the knowledge of the truth" (2 Tim. 3:7).

Don't be like the one who superficially and carelessly chooses a section of the world's sand to build his hope on. Instead, be concerned about the depth of spiritual reward that comes with wisely considering and carefully choosing God's solid foundation.

AUGUST 29

THE WISE BUILDER

He is like a man building a house,
who dug deep and laid the foundation on the rock.

LUKE 6:48

The person who is wise spiritually, who is a true Christian, builds his life and performs his duties carefully, realizing the great substance and importance involved. He or she is not satisfied with a superficial profession of faith or with the shallow methods and easy shortcuts that so often accompany false religion.

Knowing that the Lord is due all credit, praise, and worship, the wise builder will want to give Him maximum effort and diligent service. This person knows that everything truly done for Christ is done out of love, not out of compulsion or fear. So serve the Lord with gladness and be a wise builder in His kingdom.

AUTHORITATIVE TEACHING

The people were astonished at His teaching,
for He taught them as one having authority.

MATTHEW 7:28–29

One fact that struck Jesus' audiences as much as any other was that He was an authoritative teacher. The most predominant New Testament word used for authority pertains to power and privilege and demonstrates the sovereignty of Christ.

In contrast to Jesus, the Jewish scribes quoted others to lend authority to their teachings. The Lord needed to quote only God's Word and could speak as the final authority on truth. He spoke eternal truth simply, directly, powerfully, yet with love and compassion. That astounded His hearers—and it should also profoundly impress us.

THE ULTIMATE RESPONSE

The Lord is not . . . willing that any
should perish but that all should come to repentance.

2 PETER 3:9

Amazement is an appropriate and, in fact, unavoidable response to the words and teachings of Jesus. But our response to them should not end with amazement or even serious pondering. The ultimate response to Jesus' teaching is belief and obedience. He did not expound the truths He did merely for our astonishment or information. He taught what He did for our salvation.

Many respond to Jesus by merely considering His words and actions but not embracing them. What is your ultimate response?

Security

September

ETERNAL SECURITY IS SURE

I give them eternal life, and they shall never perish;
neither shall anyone snatch them out of My hand.

JOHN 10:28

Today's verse is a wonderful promise from the Lord Jesus Himself that the believer's salvation is forever secure in Him. Furthermore, the first three words of Romans 8:28, "And we know," express the absolute certainty you can have, verified by the Holy Spirit, that you will never lose your salvation.

Based on divinely revealed authority, the apostle Paul asserts to the Roman church and to us that, as Christians, we can know beyond all doubt that we are secure in God's hands. As you walk with Him, He will display His glory in your salvation and work out everything in your sanctification for your ultimate blessing.

GOD THE GUARANTOR

My Father, who has given them to Me,
is greater than all; and no one is able to
snatch them out of My Father's hand.

JOHN 10:29

Sadly, many believers throughout church history, including many today, have refused to believe that God guarantees their eternal security. Such denial derives from the erroneous conviction that salvation is a cooperative endeavor between people and God. Such reasoning says that an almighty God will not fail to do His part, but that a fallible Christian might fail to do his part.

But belief in what Scripture says about salvation— that it comes from a sovereign God alone—will lead you to the confidence that your salvation is secure. If salvation is all of God, then you can know with certainty that He will not fail to secure it. Anyone who is truly God's child need never fear losing his citizenship in heaven. And if that describes you, you can surely trust Christ's words from today's verse that "no one is able to snatch them out of My Father's hand."

SECURITY HAS NO LIMITS

He is also able to save to the
uttermost those who come to God through Him.

HEBREWS 7:25

The extent of your security as a believer is as limitless as its certainty is absolute. In fact, the expression "to the uttermost" in today's verse literally means "completely," or "forever." The security of salvation is utterly comprehensive, without qualifications or limits.

The Father's infallible decree of security for Christians was graciously and completely carried out through the work of His Son at Calvary (see 1 John 2:1). And that security is strong enough to last throughout your entire life on earth, until you are in the presence of the Lord. The apostle Jude offers this encouraging benediction, which you can always count on: "Now to Him who is able to keep you from stumbling, and to present you faultless before the presence of His glory with exceeding joy" (Jude 24).

GOD'S PROVIDENCE

*All things work together for good
to those who love God.*

ROMANS 8:28

God regularly and consistently takes all that He allows to happen to Christians, even what seems to them to be the worst things, and turns those events ultimately into blessings. That is divine providence at work.

No matter what your situation—happy, prosperous, and easy; or sad, painful, and difficult—through it all, God works to do what is ultimately best and most blessed for you.

In His providence, the Lord uses "all things," circumstances that are evil and harmful as well as those that are good and helpful, to mold you into the kind of person He wants you to be. When you struggle with life, just remember what God promised the apostle Paul, "'My grace is sufficient for you, for My strength is made perfect in weakness'" (2 Cor. 12:9). That pledge is for you as well.

WHEN DOES GOOD COME?

All the paths of the Lord are mercy and truth,
to such as keep His covenant and His testimonies.

PSALM 25:10

After delivering the Israelites from slavery in Egypt, God continually guided them through the harsh obstacles of the Sinai desert. Moses reminded them: "'[God] led you through the great and terrible wilderness, in which were fiery serpents and scorpions and thirsty land where there was no water . . . that He might humble you and that He might test you, to do you good in the end'" (Deut. 8:15–16).

That illustration, along with many others from Scripture, clearly demonstrates that the Lord often delays the good He has promised to His own. God certainly didn't lead the Israelites through forty years of challenging tests only to bring them to an evil end. Instead, He brought them good, even though He used a large amount of discipline and refining to accomplish it.

As Christians, we also can expect temporal hardships before realizing the final glory God has waiting for us. Paul reminds us that "our light affliction, which is but for a moment, is working for us a far more exceeding and eternal weight of glory" (2 Cor. 4:17).

THE GOODNESS OF GOD'S POWER

The Lord is slow to anger and great in power.

NAHUM 1:3

God's power, one of His primary attributes, is often on display for our good. It supports us in our troubles and strengthens our spiritual life. Near the end of his life, Moses told God's people, "'The eternal God is your refuge, and underneath are the everlasting arms'" (Deut. 33:27).

In His parting words to the disciples, just prior to His ascension, Jesus promised, "'But you shall receive power when the Holy Spirit has come upon you; and you shall be witnesses to Me in Jerusalem, and in all Judea and Samaria, and to the end of the earth'" (Acts 1:8).

Whether our outward circumstances are favorable or unfavorable, these and other divine promises about God's power are there for us to claim.

THE GOODNESS
OF GOD'S WISDOM

This also comes from the Lord of hosts,
Who is wonderful in counsel and excellent in guidance.

ISAIAH 28:29

The most direct way we see the goodness of God's wisdom is when He shares it with us. The apostle Paul prayed that He would grant to believers in Ephesus and everywhere "the spirit of wisdom and revelation in the knowledge of Him" (Eph. 1:17). He expressed similar sentiments in his letter to the Colossians: "We . . . do not cease to pray for you, and to ask that you may be filled with the knowledge of His will in all wisdom and spiritual understanding" (1:9); "Let the word of Christ dwell in you richly in all wisdom, teaching and admonishing one another in psalms and hymns and spiritual songs, singing with grace in your hearts to the Lord" (3:16).

How are you doing in utilizing the goodness of God's wisdom?

THE GOODNESS
OF GOD'S FAITHFULNESS

Through the Lord's mercies we are not consumed,
because His compassions fail not. They are new
every morning; great is Your faithfulness.

LAMENTATIONS 3:22–23

The goodness of God's faithfulness to believers is apparent, because even when we are unfaithful to Him, He remains faithful to us. The prophet Micah rejoiced in God's faithfulness, exulting, "Who is a God like You, pardoning iniquity and passing over the transgression of the remnant of His heritage? He does not retain His anger forever, because He delights in mercy" (Mic. 7:18).

Whenever you're in need, you can rely on the faithfulness of God's promises, such as these: "He shall call upon Me, and I will answer him; I will be with him in trouble; I will deliver him and honor him" (Ps. 91:15); "And my God shall supply all your need according to His riches in glory by Christ Jesus" (Phil. 4:19).

THE INTRINSICALLY GOOD

Whatever things are of good report,
if there is any virtue and if there is anything
praiseworthy—meditate on these things.

PHILIPPIANS 4:8

Almost by definition, certain things in the spiritual realm are good. First, God Himself is good. "Or do you despise the riches of His goodness, forbearance, and longsuffering, not knowing that the goodness of God leads you to repentance?" (Rom. 2:4).

Second, God's Word is good and works for our good. Paul told the Ephesian elders, "'I commend you to God and to the word of His grace, which is able to build you up and give you an inheritance among all those who are sanctified'" (Acts 20:32).

Third, God's holy angels are good and are there to support believers. The writer of Hebrews affirms this with the rhetorical question, "Are they not all ministering spirits sent forth to minister for those who will inherit salvation?" (Heb. 1:14).

These are truths not only worth meditating on but, in view of their realities, living out.

MINISTERS TO ONE ANOTHER

*Let us consider one another
in order to stir up love and good works.*

HEBREWS 10:24

 God wants His children to minister His good to one another. Paul the apostle, as he opened his letter to the Roman believers, assured them that he was eager to visit them not only to minister *to* them, but to be ministered to *by* them: ". . . that I may be encouraged together with you by the mutual faith both of you and me" (Rom. 1:12). Before that, he had described Timothy and himself to the Corinthians as "fellow workers for your joy" (2 Cor. 1:24).

If you're truly a follower of Christ, it should be both an obligation and a joy for you to encourage other believers toward love and good works, as today's verse instructs.

IS EVIL EVER GOOD?

You meant evil against me;
but God meant it for good.

GENESIS 50:20

As difficult as it is to accept or many times even recognize, God sometimes allows evil things to work for the good of believers. Many of the things you do or that happen to you are either evil or, at best, worthless. Yet the Lord in His infinite wisdom and power can and does turn the worst of such things to your ultimate good.

The famous account of Daniel in the lions' den is a great illustration of how evil can be turned into good. When Daniel did not substitute worship of King Darius for worship of the true God, the king ordered him thrown into the pit of lions. When the lions would not harm him, Daniel declared to Darius, "'O king, live forever! My God sent His angel and shut the lions' mouths, so that they have not hurt me, because I was found innocent before Him; and also, O king, I have done no wrong before you'" (Dan. 6:21–22). Daniel was such a testimony to the king of how God could use evil for good that he happily released Daniel and gave praise to the Lord.

CAN SUFFERING BE GOOD?

*Blessed be the God and Father of our
Lord Jesus Christ, the Father of mercies and God of
all comfort, who comforts us in all our tribulation.*

2 CORINTHIANS 1:3–4

We often don't pause to consider that God can turn the evil of suffering into a lesson for good, a lesson we can use to grow spiritually. Sometimes suffering in the form of persecution comes simply because we do not want to compromise our faithfulness to the Lord. Many other times it is merely the common pain, hardship, disease, and conflicts resulting from sin's corruption of the world.

Sometimes, however, God does bring suffering as a means to discipline us when we fall into a pattern of sin. That's what happened to Ananias and Sapphira in the early church (see Acts 5:1–11). Similarly, God punished some members of the Corinthian church for their flagrant sins (1 Cor. 11:29–30).

Whatever the case, you do not have to view suffering as bad. It can teach you kindness, sympathy, humility, compassion, patience, and gentleness. Most important, God can use suffering in unique ways to draw you closer to Him.

LOVE FOR GOD

"You shall love the Lord your God with all your heart, with all your soul, with all your mind, and with all your strength." This is the first commandment.

MARK 12:30

In addition to the words of Jesus in today's verse, other New Testament books make it clear that believers are to love God. Paul wrote to the Corinthians, quoting from the prophet Isaiah, "'Eye has not seen, nor ear heard, nor have entered into the heart of man the things which God has prepared for those who love Him'" (1 Cor. 2:9). Elsewhere the apostle refers to Christians as "those who love our Lord Jesus Christ in sincerity" (Eph. 6:24).

Sincere love for God is the first mark of genuine saving faith. That is true "because the love of God has been poured out in our hearts by the Holy Spirit who was given to us" (Rom. 5:5). In view of all this, it's no accident that Paul lists love as the first aspect of the Spirit's fruit (Gal. 5:22).

CHARACTERISTICS OF LOVE FOR GOD

This is my prayer:
that your love may abound more and more.

PHILIPPIANS 1:9, NIV

 Genuine love for God has many facets. Here is a list of the most important ones.

• It longs for personal communion with God (Pss. 42:1–2; 73:25).
• It trusts in God's power to protect His own (Ps. 31:23).
• It is characterized by peace that only God can impart (Ps. 119:165; John 14:27).
• It is sensitive to God's will and His honor (Ps. 69:9).
• It loves the people God loves (1 John 4:7–8, 20–21).
• It hates what God hates (1 John 2:15).
• It longs for the Second Coming of Christ (2 Tim. 4:8).

Finally, and most important, it is marked by obedience to God (John 14:21; 1 John 5:1–2).

We are able to love God and manifest these facets only because He first loved us (1 John 4:7, 10, 19). Do you love God?

THE CALLED OF GOD

Those who are the called according to His purpose.

ROMANS 8:28

The New Testament epistles use the terms *called* and *calling* in reference to the sovereign, regenerating work of God in a believer's heart that brings him to new life in Christ. All the called of God are chosen and redeemed by Him and are ultimately glorified. He has securely predestined them to be His children and to be conformed to the image of His Son.

Although human faith is essential if we are to be among the called, it is even more essential that God initiate our calling to salvation. God's choice not only precedes man's choice but makes man's choice possible and effective. "'No one can come to Me [Christ] unless it has been granted to him by My Father'" (John 6:65).

Primarily, God's call to the redeemed is once and for all. But secondarily, it continues until the Christian is finally glorified. That ought to thrill us and motivate us to emulate Paul's resolve to "press toward the goal for the prize of the upward call of God in Christ Jesus" (Phil. 3:14).

GOD'S DIVINE PURPOSE

*He chose us in Him before the
foundation of the world, that we should be holy
and without blame before Him in love.*

EPHESIANS 1:4

While Israel was still wandering in the desert of Sinai, Moses told them, "The Lord did not set His love on you or choose you because you were more in number than any other people, for you were the least of all peoples; but because the Lord loves you, and because He would keep the oath which He swore to your fathers, the Lord has brought you out with a mighty hand, and redeemed you from the house of bondage, from the hand of Pharaoh king of Egypt" (Deut. 7:7–8). God did not choose the Jews because of who they were but because of who He is.

The same is true of God's choosing believers. He chooses solely on the basis of His divine will, purpose, and love. There's nothing you did to earn or gain salvation; it's all of God. Be thankful that He chose you from before the foundations of the world.

TARNISHING THE IMAGE

Love your enemies, bless those who curse you, do good to those who hate you, and pray for those who spitefully use you and persecute you, that you may be sons of your Father in heaven.
MATTHEW 5:44–45

When I was a little boy, a friend and I once got into trouble when we were caught stealing some things from a store. The police took us to the city jail. At the time, my father was out playing golf with some deacons from our church. He was notified about what had happened and came to the jail thinking a mistake had been made. Then he had to explain to the deacons what his son was doing in jail.

When I got home, my mother was crying because she thought I would never do such a thing. Someone told me, "Johnny MacArthur, have you forgotten who your father is?" I never forgot that statement. I owed something to my father. He had given me my very life, and I was happy to be his son. I'm also glad to be my heavenly Father's son, so it's only right that I manifest something of His character.

A DESIRE TO OBEY

*Though you were slaves of sin, yet you obeyed from
the heart that form of doctrine to which you were delivered.*

ROMANS 6:17

If I were to define the Christian life with one word, I would choose the word *obedience*. Obedience, power, blessing, and joy are four legs to the same chair; they are essential elements of the Christian life. Without obedience, there will be no power, blessing, or joy in our lives.

One key distinction between a true Christian and someone who merely professes to be a Christian is a heartfelt desire to obey God. For a Christian, *obedience* is a sweet, hopeful, and encouraging word. It ought to be a welcome expression of the deepest desire of your heart. If you are willing to obey God, and your desire to do so comes out of love not fear, that is a good indication that you are a true child of God.

BOUND TO OBEY

That the righteous requirement
of the law might be fulfilled in us who do not
walk according to the flesh but according to the Spirit.

ROMANS 8:4

Some people believe that since we are saved by grace and are no longer under the law, then we are no longer bound to the law. That's true in this sense: we are not bound to the penalty of the law. Since we came to Christ, the law no longer has power to condemn or execute us. However, we are bound to its precepts, for God has not changed His morality.

The apostle Paul said, "There is therefore now no condemnation to those who are in Christ Jesus. . . . For the law of the Spirit of life in Christ Jesus has made me free from the law of sin and death. For what the law could not do in that it was weak through the flesh, God did by sending His Son in the likeness of sinful flesh, on account of sin: He condemned sin in the flesh" (Rom. 8:1–3). The sacrifice of Christ freed us from the penalty of the law—He died in our place. So we are free from the law only in the sense that it cannot condemn us, yet we are still commanded to obey its precepts.

HOPE IN THE BATTLE

With the mind I serve the law of God,
but with the flesh the law of sin.

ROMANS 7:25

 Since Christians are called to obedience and the new nature longs to obey, what do you do when you are tempted to disobey? For one thing, you have the power of the Holy Spirit in you (Rom. 8:2), who enables you to do the will of God. But Paul also describes the reality of our ongoing battle with the flesh in Romans 7. He says, "I see another law in my members, warring against the law of my mind" (v. 23).

The sin principle in our humanness wars against our desire to obey. Every Christian fights that battle. Your humanness wars against the new creation that delights in the law of God. What gives us hope is that the longer we fight the battle, the more victorious we will be. So thank the Lord for continuing His work to deliver you and give you victory each day from sin.

THE DEBT OF LOVE

Owe no one anything except to love one another.

ROMANS 13:8

Christians owe love to everyone in society. Jesus said, "By this all will know that you are My disciples, if you have love for one another" (John 13:35). Our love to one another applies first of all to fellow believers, our brothers and sisters in Christ.

But one another also applies to unbelievers—all unbelievers, not just those who are likeable and friendly. Jesus said, "Love your enemies, bless those who curse you, do good to those who hate you, and pray for those who spitefully use you" (Matt. 5:44). The apostle Paul said, "Let us do good to all, especially to those who are of the household of faith" (Gal. 6:10).

Love should be a distinctive trait in your life. You owe the debt to everyone, so make sure you show love to everyone so you will be known as someone who loves "one another fervently with a pure heart" (1 Pet. 1:22).

DEMONSTRATING LOVE

Walk in love.

EPHESIANS 5:2

What is love? How do you demonstrate it? To be able to practice love, you need to know what it is biblically. Throughout Scripture, love is characterized as an action.

First of all, love teaches the truth to others (Eph. 4:15) and ministers to their needs (Heb. 6:10). It sets an example by serving others and stimulating them to grow (Gal. 5:13). It covers other people's faults (1 Pet. 4:8) and forgives (Eph. 4:32). Love also endures the problems and idiosyncrasies of others (1 Cor. 13:7) and sacrifices on their behalf (John 15:13–14).

Self-sacrificial love gives spiritual truth, help, and concern to those in need. We owe everyone that kind of love and should not owe anything else. That's the heart of Christian living; it's the magnet that attracts the world.

SUBMIT TO THE SPIRIT

The love of God has been poured out in
our hearts by the Holy Spirit who was given to us.

ROMANS 5:5

You need to give the Holy Spirit complete control over your life. You can either hold onto feelings of bitterness, anxiety, and hatred toward someone, or you can yield them to the Spirit of God. When you submit to the Holy Spirit, He takes over your life and replaces bitterness with love and vengeance with affection. Paul said, "Concerning brotherly love you have no need that I should write to you, for you yourselves are taught by God to love one another" (1 Thess. 4:9).

The capacity to love others is available within you; you just need to understand the resource. If you submit to the Holy Spirit, He will teach you how to love.

A CONSCIOUS CHOICE

Above all things put on love,
which is the bond of perfection.

COLOSSIANS 3:14

All believers need to make a conscious choice to love others. Some time ago I counseled a couple who had been struggling seriously in their marriage for quite a while. I shared with them that they needed to make a conscious choice to love each other. They had to train themselves to love at times when they felt angry or taken advantage of. They needed to replace rudeness and unkind words with love.

Two days after our talk, the husband called me and said, "I just wanted to let you know that each time a problem arises, we are endeavoring to do all we can in the Spirit of God to make a conscious choice to love, make peace, and show kindness no matter what the price to our own ego might be." Choosing to be kind to others and forgive them is a factor in learning how to love. The Holy Spirit enables you to do that when you train your mind and make a commitment to obey the Lord.

An Inexhaustible Reservoir

You have purified your souls
in obeying the truth through the Spirit
in sincere love of the brethren.

1 PETER 1:22

As Christians we have a great responsibility to love others, but how do we fulfill it? By understanding our resource.

Love is available to us, and it's our fault if we don't tap the necessary resource. We are to submit to the Spirit and learn how to love. We must purify our hearts by confessing our sin and realize the urgency of attracting others to Christ through our love. We are to make a conscious choice to love others, fellowship with other believers, and concentrate on others rather than ourselves. And we must consider the effect of loving others. Love given is inevitably returned.

When God saved you, He made you a new creation with the capacity to fulfill the debt of love. The reservoir of love is inexhaustible. You have the privilege of representing God in the world by loving others as He loved them and receiving love in return.

AN ASSIGNMENT ON LOVE

Know the love of Christ which passes knowledge.

EPHESIANS 3:19

 To pay the debt of love, we can all do several things. Here are some suggestions:

Mend a quarrel.

Call a friend you haven't seen for a long time.

Replace a suspicion with a trust.

Remove any bitterness in your life.

Write a surprise letter to someone who loves you.

Tell someone you know well how much he or she means to you.

Keep a promise.

Ask God to forgive someone who did something wrong to you, and forget the wrongdoing.

Don't be overly demanding on the other members of your family.

Express thanks to others throughout the day.

Tell someone you love that you care.

Pray for one of your enemies.

Send a check to someone who has a need.

Ask God to help you to love the way Jesus loved.

FULFILLING THE LAW

Love does no harm to a neighbor;
therefore love is the fulfillment of the law.

ROMANS 13:9

The key to obeying the law of God is love. When we love others, we will automatically obey the law. You won't commit adultery if you love someone. That's because love doesn't defile others or steal purity. Only lust and selfishness do that. If you love someone, your love renders useless the command not to kill. I don't need to be reminded not to kill people if I love them. When you love someone, you won't steal from him either. Therefore you don't need to be told not to steal. Nor will you covet what someone else has when you love him.

Love doesn't replace the law; it fulfills the law. Through love, you can fulfill God's love.

OBEYING OUT OF LOVE

*The purpose of the commandment
is love from a pure heart.*

1 TIMOTHY 1:5

The keeping of a commandment should flow from a heart of love. It's possible to obey the law out of fear and to be afraid of God's punishment. But when you do that, you don't really obey the law in the fullest sense because fear is not the biblical motive for obedience. Fear will restrain you from some evil and its effect can be somewhat productive, but its result is incomplete.

Some keep the law out of self-interest. They believe that if they live a moral life, God will repay them. But that is not a pure motive for obedience—it's a selfish one. Although you may restrain yourself from evil and do good things outwardly, you won't have an obedience that comes from an attitude of love. The true intention of the law is to cultivate love from the heart. That's how the law is fulfilled.

LOVE ME, LOVE MEN

*On these two commandments
hang all the Law and the Prophets.*

MATTHEW 22:40

Jesus said that the Ten Commandments could be summed up in two commands: love Me, and love men. Perhaps you wonder how you can ever live up to all the commands in the Bible. The answer is very simple: love God, love men, and do what you want.

When you love God with all your heart, soul, mind, and strength, and you love your neighbor as yourself, you can do what you want because you will be the person God wants you to be. Because of your love, you won't kill anyone, defile anyone, steal anything, or covet what another person has. The Spirit will cultivate in your heart a love that precludes any desire to do wrong.

WHO IS YOUR NEIGHBOR?

"You shall love your neighbor as yourself."

ROMANS 13:9

When Paul says we are to love our neighbors as ourselves, he means that we should have the same care and concern for others that we have for ourselves. Paul said the same thing in this way: "Let each of you look not only for his own interests, but also for the interests of others" (Phil. 2:4). You should be just as concerned about the comfort, happiness, peace, and joy of others as you are about your own.

Whose face do you wash in the morning? Whose hair do you comb? Whose wardrobe do you buy? Whose comforts are you concerned about? You are concerned about your self-preservation and self-comfort and should be concerned about others in the same way. Pay as much attention to them as you do yourself. That's loving your neighbor as yourself.

Who is your neighbor? Anyone who comes across your path. Although it is hard to love everyone, you have a new capacity within you to do that (Rom. 5:5).

Endurance

OCTOBER

Job's Confession

I have uttered what I did not understand,
things too wonderful for me, which I did not know.

Job 42:3

At difficult times in our lives, God can seem distant or disinterested in our plight. That's because our human emotions can override trust in God's truth, and we can come to believe that no desirable outcome to our present situation exists.

Job, however, shows us that with endurance and patience we can learn whatever lessons God wants us to learn. It was that very trust that caused him to glorify God at the conclusion to his time of suffering: "I have heard of You by the hearing of the ear, but now my eye sees You. Therefore I abhor myself, and repent in dust and ashes"(Job 42:5–6).

As a result of patience and unwavering trust during his long ordeal, Job gained a new understanding of his sovereign God and a greater reassurance of the joys of being dealt with as one of His children.

ABRAHAM'S FAITH

By faith Abraham, when he was tested,
offered up Isaac, and he who had received the promises
offered up his only begotten son, of whom it was said,
"In Isaac your seed be called," concluding that God
was able to raise him up, even from the dead.

HEBREWS 11:17-19

 Abraham's obedience took a tremendous amount of faith. He was willing to obey God because he believed God could raise the dead, even though he had never before seen the dead raised to life. He believed God was so true to His Word and character that if He made a promise, He would even raise the dead to keep it. Is it any wonder he is the greatest human model of faith?

The apostle Paul also commented on Abraham's faith: "Those who are of faith are sons of Abraham. . . . Those who are of faith are blessed with believing Abraham" (Gal. 3:7, 9). Anyone who lives by faith in God is in a spiritual sense a son of Abraham. He is the father of the faithful. The account of Abraham tells us that a man can go through the severest trial of life imaginable if he trusts God, believing that He will keep His promise and accomplish His purposes without making a mistake.

OCTOBER 3

No Fool's Paradise

Yea, though I walk through the valley
of the shadow of death, I will fear no evil;
for You are with me.

PSALM 23:4

We have to realize that God is going to allow us to go through tests and that He is working all things out for His own holy purpose (Rom. 8:28). I know we all dream of a perfect environment of comfort and tranquility. Although any temporary rest from trials may lead us into believing we might find permanent exemption from them, our lives on earth will never be free from trials. We can live in a fool's paradise, never forecasting any trouble and predicting a future of ease, but that is a fantasy. Christ warned His disciples and all who follow in His footsteps to expect trials in this life (John 15:18–16:6).

Puritan Thomas Manton once observed that God had one Son without sin, but no Son without a cross. As Christians, we can be assured that we will have trials. But our confidence is that we will have victory over them through the presence of God. Trials will come, but God's grace will meet us in our time of need.

WHAT'S IN YOUR HEART?

God withdrew from him [King Hezekiah],
in order to test him, that He might know
all that was in his heart.

2 CHRONICLES 32:31

God didn't need to test Hezekiah to know what was in his heart. God already knew by omniscience. But He tests us so we can find out. He assists us in doing a spiritual inventory on ourselves by bringing trials into our lives to demonstrate the strength or weakness of our faith. If you're currently experiencing a trial and are shaking your fist at God and wondering why it's happening, that's a good indication that you have weak faith. If, on the other hand, you're resting and rejoicing in the Lord, having placed the trial into His care, then you have strong faith.

Weaned from the World

*[Moses esteemed] the reproach of Christ
greater riches than the treasures in Egypt;
for he looked to the reward.*

Hebrews 11:26

The longer we live, the more we accumulate. But those things tend to hold less significance for Christians. When trials come into your life and you reach out for those worldly things, you see what little lasting difference they make. Trials can wean you away from worldly things as they demonstrate their utter inability to solve any problem or provide any resource in a time of stress.

Moses learned the value of trials even though he had been raised in Pharaoh's house as a prince of Egypt. As part of the royal family, he had the best education and reached the apex of Egyptian society in terms of wealth, honor, and comfort. But he considered the sacrifices made in identifying with God's purposes "greater riches than the treasures in Egypt." He took his eyes off all of the worldly things available to him and began to be concerned about the trials of his people, which the Lord used to wean him away from material pleasures.

THE WATER TEST

*We also glory in tribulations, knowing that
tribulation produces perseverance; and perseverance,
character; and character, hope.*

ROMANS 5:3–4

Jewelers use "the water test" as one of the surest ways to identify a true diamond. An imitation stone is never as brilliant as a genuine stone, but sometimes the difference can't be determined with the unaided eye. Jewelers know that a genuine diamond placed in water sparkles brilliantly, whereas the sparkle of the imitation is practically extinguished. That test makes picking the real diamond relatively easy.

By way of analogy, I find that the faith of many people under the water of sorrow or affliction is nothing but an imitation. However, when a true child of God is immersed in a trial, he will shine as brilliantly as ever.

THE JOY THAT AWAITS

My brethren, count it all joy
when you fall into various trials.

JAMES 1:2

The joy we experience from our trials can be some of the greatest joy we know. Since one of the major reasons God sends trials into our lives is to test the genuineness of our faith, what more fitting occasion to have joy than in and after an experience of suffering that has proved the reality of our salvation? A strengthened assurance of our salvation and confidence that God cares for us, as manifest in the reality that our suffering could neither break our faith nor sever us from His love, is cause for the highest happiness.

True joy does not come cheaply or as a fleeting, superficial emotion. Real joy is produced by much deeper factors than the circumstances that produce superficial happiness. If you are struggling through the negative circumstances of life, floundering in doubt and dismay, you have forgotten that genuine joy resides in the confidence that your life is hidden with Christ in God. In God's providence, that joy and assurance can be most strong during a trial.

HAPPY TRIALS

We count them blessed who endure.

JAMES 5:11

James ended his discourse on trials by saying, "Blessed is the man who endures temptation [trials]" (1:12). People who successfully endure trials and overcome temptation are truly happy. James is not saying that happiness comes in freedom from trials but in victory over them. There is a big difference. It's not the shallow joy of the spectator who never experienced conflict; it's the exuberance of the participant who fought and won. Is your experience the former or the latter?

ENDURING TO THE END

Blessed is the man who
endures temptation [trials].

JAMES 1:12

The word *endurance* in today's verse speaks of patiently and triumphantly enduring. It connotes passive or even painful survival and focuses on the outcome of being victorious. The person who goes through trials and comes out a winner never gives up his faith or abandons God. He is shown to be the genuine article.

Some people come to church, profess Christ, and even get baptized. Yet when trouble comes into their lives, they're gone. And they may never come back. Maybe they encountered a broken relationship, the death of a loved one, or some other struggle, and the circumstances were so overpowering that they blamed God and walked away, convinced that Christianity doesn't work.

As believers, we may experience times of struggle and doubt, but our faith will never be destroyed. We cling to the Lord despite our trials because we love Him. That kind of loving perseverance results in true blessing.

REST YOUR HOPE

*Rest your hope fully on the grace that is
brought to you at the revelation of Jesus Christ.*

1 PETER 1:13

You've heard plenty of sermons and seen plenty of books on love and faith, but have you ever heard a message or read a book on hope? For some reason, we often ignore hope. Hope is a missing element in the Christian experience of our culture. We don't live in hope primarily because we focus too much on our present circumstances.

What is hope? It is the Christian's attitude toward the future. Hope in its essence is like faith. Both have trust, or a belief in God, as their focus, but there's a difference between them. Faith is believing God in the present, and hope is believing God for the future. Faith believes God for what He has done, and hope believes God for what He will do.

Fix your hope on Him and live in anticipation of the glorious fulfillment of His future promise.

OCTOBER 11

Our Future Crown

When he has been approved,
he will receive the crown of life.

JAMES 1:12

Eternal life is the crown that God has promised
to those who love Him. It is the believer's ultimate reward. Although we presently experience some
of the benefits of eternal life, we possess it on promise;
some day we will receive it in its fullness. We are still
waiting to enter into our future reward. At the Lord's
coming, He will grant to us the fullness of eternal life.

The apostle Paul expressed a similar thought:
"Finally, there is laid up for me the crown of
righteousness, which the Lord, the righteous Judge, will
give to me on that Day, and not to me only but also to
all who have loved His appearing" (2 Tim. 4:8). When
Christ returns for the church, Christians will be granted
a life of eternal righteousness. We will all receive the
same crown consisting of the rewards of eternal life,
righteousness, and glory.

Endurance does not earn eternal life. However,
endurance is the proof of true faith and love, and that
is rewarded by the fullness of eternal life.

A WELCOME FRIEND

No chastening seems to be joyful for the present,
but painful; nevertheless, afterward it yields the peaceable fruit
of righteousness to those who have been trained by it.

HEBREWS 12:11

Evaluating a trial as a joyful occurrence is something a Christian must discipline himself to do, because joy is not the natural human response to troubles. He must make a conscious commitment to face each trial with a joyous attitude. Paul was a prisoner in Rome when he said to the Philippians, "Rejoice in the Lord always. Again I say, rejoice. . . . I have learned in whatever state I am, to be content" (4:4, 11). He had learned to be content and rejoice in the midst of trials. That's not something that happens by accident.

When you see a trial coming, take on an attitude of joy that comes from anticipating the perfecting work the Lord will do through it. We must have a decisive conviction that we are going to face trials with a joyful attitude. It is the joy of one who counts it a privilege to have his faith tested because he knows the testing will draw him closer to the Savior. Then a trial will become a welcome friend.

A CAPTIVE AUDIENCE

All the saints greet you,
but especially those who are of Caesar's household.

PHILIPPIANS 4:22

Not all suffering is physical. Sometimes we go through emotional and mental suffering. Paul was a prisoner in Rome when he wrote to the Philippians. His ministry had been greatly curtailed; nevertheless, he told the Philippians that his imprisonment had actually aided the furtherance of the gospel. Being chained to Roman soldiers, he had the opportunity to win them to the Lord (v. 13).

There was a revival of sorts taking place in Caesar's palace, which evidently led to the salvation of some, as today's verse indicates. The soldiers didn't know who they had on their hands: they believed they had a prisoner, but in reality they had a self-appointed evangelist to whom they were a captive audience! What a model of rejoicing in the midst of a potentially frustrating and discouraging situation!

GAINING AN
UNDERSTANDING MIND

*Knowing that the testing
of your faith produces patience.*

JAMES 1:3

Don't ever doubt that trials will accomplish something positive. They are designed to produce "patience," or—better translated—"endurance" or "perseverance." With every trial, we build the tenacity of spirit that holds on under pressure while waiting patiently on God to remove the trial at the appointed time and then reward us. It strengthens us as we gain more endurance.

God builds us up in the same way a runner gradually develops the ability to run long distance. He starts small and works up to his maximum capacity. God allows increasingly greater trials in our lives to increase our endurance for greater ministry and joy, for the more difficult the battle, the sweeter the victory. When you come out of a difficult trial, you can rejoice over God's delivering you. That proves Him to be trustworthy, and that strengthens your faith.

WAITING FOR HEAVEN

We ourselves groan within ourselves,
eagerly waiting for the adoption, the redemption
of our body, for we were saved in this hope.

ROMANS 8:23–24

Trials in a believer's life increase his anticipation for heaven. Just as trials create a growing disinterest in the passing world, they also create a greater desire, for example, to be reunited with a loved one who has gone to be with the Lord. If the most beloved people in your life have entered into the presence of our precious Savior, and if you have invested your time and money in eternal things, then you won't have much tying you to this passing world.

Beyond this life of suffering is a glorious future for the believer that makes us all the more desirous for the fulfillment of salvation. Thus trials give us a greater affection for that which is eternal—they help us long for the eternal city of heaven.

EXERCISING FAITH

For we live by faith, not by sight.

2 CORINTHIANS 5:7

Thomas Manton said that while all things are quiet and comfortable, we live by sense rather than faith. But the worth of a soldier is never known in times of peace. It is always a challenge to stay focused properly through a difficult trial. Even with the promise of lessons learned and rewards realized, the certainty of these benefits can seem more theoretical than real. But we can have a much greater confidence in the reality of all these things if we simply remember the words of today's verse.

One of God's purposes in trials is to give us greater strength. As you go through one trial, your spiritual muscles (faith) are exercised and strengthened for the next one. That means you can face greater foes and endure greater obstacles, thus becoming more useful to the Lord. And the more useful you are, the more you will accomplish His will in the power of His Spirit for His glory.

OCTOBER 17

WISDOM FROM GOD

If any of you lacks wisdom, let him ask of God.

JAMES 1:5

When you are being tested, you need to recognize your need for strength, and you must look for a greater resource to hold onto in the midst of the trial—God Himself. The search for wisdom is man's supreme search. For those who know and love the Lord, He provides that wisdom.

This kind of wisdom is not philosophical speculation, but the absolutes of God's will—the divine wisdom that is pure and peaceable (James 3:17). Divine wisdom results in right conduct in all of life's matters. When some Christians go through troubles, their first response is to run to some other human resource. Although God may work through other believers, your initial response to trials should be to ask God directly for wisdom that will allow you to be joyous and submissive in finding and carrying out God's will.

Today's verse is a command to pray. It is as mandatory as Paul's instruction to "pray without ceasing" (1 Thess. 5:17). Trials are intended to drive us to dependency on God by making us realize we have no sufficient human resources.

ASK FOR WISDOM

For the Lord gives wisdom.

PROVERBS 2:6

 I believe God will provide the wisdom to understand any trial if we will ask Him. If we don't ask, the Lord may allow the trial to continue until we demonstrate that we have learned to be dependent on Him through the trial.

If you lack wisdom, you're commanded to ask God for it. Wisdom is never withheld from a believer who needs it and asks for it as he perseveres through a trial. Isn't that a wonderful promise? Sometimes we don't ask; we do everything but ask God. We ought to be on our knees crying out from our hearts for God to give us His direction.

ASKING IN FAITH

But let him ask in faith, with no doubting.

JAMES 1:6

A believer should request wisdom in confident trust in God. If you lack wisdom, it's not God's fault. If you don't understand your trial—why your spouse died, your health is deteriorating, your finances are a mess, or why you are having problems with your car, your job, or your children—then you probably haven't asked God with unwavering faith to give you wisdom.

Perhaps you have prayed somewhat insincerely with wrong motives like those whom James condemned as praying for wisdom only to help with their lusts (4:3). Maybe you're not praying in accord with 1 Timothy 2:8, which says to pray "without wrath or doubting," and you doubt whether God is able or willing to help.

Unwavering faith simply believes that God is a sovereign, loving God who will supply everything needed for understanding the trial and being able to endure it. Whatever the trial is, you can believe that God allowed it for His purpose and your spiritual maturity.

WITHOUT A DOUBT

*He who doubts is like a wave of the sea driven
and tossed by the wind. For let not that man suppose
that he will receive anything from the Lord.*

JAMES 1:6–7

The doubting person who doesn't believe that
God can provide wisdom is like the billowing,
restless sea, moving back and forth with its endless tides,
never able to settle. There's no sense in such a person
supposing he will receive anything from the Lord.

When faced with a trial, an unbeliever who
professes to know Christ will doubt God and get angry
with Him and eventually sever his association with a
church. A true Christian who is spiritually immature
may respond in a similar manner because he reacts
emotionally to his difficult circumstances and doesn't
fully trust God. In the midst of a trial, he will not
experience a joyous attitude, an understanding mind, a
submissive will, or a believing heart. He will seem
unable to ask for wisdom from God and unwilling to
take advantage of the resources He has provided, never
knowing the resolution available to him through
faithful, persistent prayer to God.

EXALTING THE POOR

Let the lowly brother
glory in his exaltation.

JAMES 1:8

Today's verse is a command for the poor Christian to rejoice. A Christian who is economically poor may have nothing in the material world to rejoice about, but he can rejoice in the knowledge that God is exalting him spiritually in his standing before God. He may be hungry, but he has the Bread of Life. He may be thirsty, but he has the Living Water. He may be poor, but he has eternal riches. He may not have a satisfying home here, but he has a glorious home in the life to come. In this life he may have trials, but God is using them to perfect and exalt him spiritually.

The Christian who is deprived can accept his trials because of the hope of receiving an incorruptible and undefiled inheritance that will never fade away (1 Pet. 1:4). True riches belong to us, so poverty is a short-lived trial that can be endured as we look ahead to a glorious time of exaltation.

HUMBLING THE RICH

The rich in his humiliation.

JAMES 1:10

Christians who don't have to experience the trials of life related to poverty can rejoice in their "humiliation," as today's verse points out. When the trials they experience help them realize that their possessions can't buy true happiness and contentment, they will understand that their dependence is on the true riches of God's grace. The rich Christian can rejoice when he learns that material blessings are only temporary and that spiritual riches are eternal.

Trials humble all believers to the same level of dependency on God. Money doesn't buy people out of their problems, although it may solve some economic ones. When you lose a daughter, son, wife, or husband, it doesn't matter how much money you have. No amount is going to buy your way out of such a trial.

Whether to the poor or the rich, trials come into life to help us humbly recognize that our resources are in God.

OCTOBER 23

BURNED UP

*As a flower of the field, he will pass away. For no sooner
has the sun risen with a burning heat than it withers the grass;
its flower falls, and its beautiful appearance perishes.
So the rich man also will fade away in his pursuits.*

JAMES 1:11

Wealthy people usually do not realize that they can't take their riches with them. Only those who have been humbled before God know that life is "a vapor that appears for a little time and then vanishes away" (James 4:14).

In today's verse, James writes about the blooming grasses and flowers of Palestine that flourish with beautiful color in February and dry up by May. James also borrows part of his illustration from Isaiah 40:6–8. The burning heat, which could refer to the scorching wind known as a sirocco, destroys the vegetation in its path. It is illustrative of the fury of death and divine judgment that put an end to the rich man's earthly life and his material possessions.

When the rich man's possessions are burned up, he will have the true riches, just as the poor man does. If you are wealthy, make sure you have a true spirit of humility and don't trust in the possessions of life.

TRIAL OR TEMPTATION?

Do not lead us into temptation.

MATTHEW 6:13

 Temptation is a common experience of every human being, Christian or not. Paul says in 1 Corinthians 10:13 that temptations are "common to man." How we deal with the battle of temptation is a mark of the genuineness of our faith or our lack of it.

The trials that the Lord allows into our lives to strengthen us can also become temptations. They can be solicitations to evil rather than a means to spiritual growth. Every difficult thing that comes into my life either strengthens me because I obey God and stay confident in His care and power, or leads me to doubt God and disobey His Word.

Every trial has the potential to become a temptation. The difference is how you respond to it.

GOD IS NOT TO BLAME

Let no one say when he is tempted, "I am tempted by God";
for God cannot be tempted by evil, nor does He tempt anyone.

JAMES 1:13

 Although some believe in the ancient idea that God is responsible for our temptation and sin, James forbids such a thought in today's verse.

James warns against rationalizing our sin and blaming God in the midst of our battle against temptation. When you are fighting temptation and near to yielding, don't make the excuse that God is tempting you.

Assuming that no one would accuse God of directly causing him to sin, James is saying that we should not even think of God as the ultimate cause of our sins. Most people don't go as far as to see God as the direct tempter, but they do believe God is indirectly to blame by having permitted the situation and the possibility of failure. But God is not the near agency of temptation, nor is He even its remote cause. Don't ever look at yourself as a victim of God's providence.

RECOGNIZING THE TRAP

Each one is tempted when he is
drawn away by his own desires and enticed.

JAMES 1:14

Temptation doesn't come from God but from within. The term *drawn away* was used in hunting contexts to describe animals being lured into traps, and *enticed* is a term used to describe catching fish with bait. Every person is tempted when the trap of sin is baited with that which appeals to his lust. A person's lust responding to enticing bait deceptively draws him away to the point where he is trapped.

What pulls us so strongly to the bait? It's not God. And it's not Satan, his demons, or the world's evil system that entice us to sin, although they bait the hook. It is our lustful nature that pulls us to take hold of it. Our flesh, our fallen nature, has a desire for evil.

From a spiritual perspective, the problem is that even though we've been redeemed and have received a new nature, we still have an enemy within. The resident passion of the flesh, not God, is responsible for our being tempted to sin.

The Birth of Sin

When desire has conceived, it gives birth to sin;
and sin, when it is full-grown, brings forth death.

JAMES 1:15

 Most people think of sin as an individual act or behavior. But today's verse says that sin is not an act; it is the result of a process.

Sin starts with desire, which is related to emotion. It begins when you desire to be satisfied by acquiring something, when you have an emotional longing to possess what you see. Temptation then affects your mind through deception. You begin to justify and rationalize your right to possess what you desire. Your mind is deceived into believing that fulfilling your lust will satisfy you and meet your needs.

Next, your will begins to plot how you're going to get what you want, and when lust is seduced (so to speak) by the baited hook, it becomes pregnant in the womb of a person's will. Finally, the act of sin occurs.

Knowing how sin is born should help you in avoiding temptation.

324   TRUTH FOR TODAY

DEALING A DEATHBLOW TO SINFUL DESIRES

Do not be deceived, my beloved brethren.

JAMES 1:16

At what point do you deal with sin? Not at the point of behavior—because then it's too late—but at the point of desire. The person who is able to control his emotional responses is able to deal effectively with sin. When being bombarded by negative emotional responses, a person with a mind that is sanctified can deactivate desires before they are activated by the will. But once they capture the will, their birth is inevitable.

You must deal with lustful emotions if you want to effectively deal with sin in your life. If you expose your emotions to the baited hook, you may find yourself getting hooked unless you take immediate action.

Preventing Desire

The weapons of our warfare are not carnal but mighty in God for pulling down strongholds, casting down arguments and every high thing that exalts itself against the knowledge of God, bringing every thought into captivity to the obedience of Christ.

2 Corinthians 10:4–5

So many things in our evil society attempt to capture our attention: movies, television, books, music, clothing, advertisements, and now the Internet—all designed to capture the emotions. For example, advertising executives know that buying is ultimately an emotional decision. Few people know or even care about the mechanics of the car being advertised, yet they are impressed if it looks like a race car, or if a pretty girl is behind the wheel, or if other kinds of emotional bait are included in the ad.

We need to guard our minds, emotions, and wills. We need to seek God's will by meditating on His Word and letting His will become ours. An unprotected, uncontrolled, and unyielded mind is going to be filled with evil desires that will result in evil deeds. We must control how our emotions and minds respond to the tempting bait they encounter.

GOD'S GOODNESS

Every good gift and every
perfect gift is from above.

JAMES 1:17

Things that come from God are good and perfect. God could never produce evil because His nature is good. Rather, He produces unending good. Whereas we possess a nature that gives rise to sin, God does not.

Why would we try to satisfy ourselves with evil desires that result in death when God is pouring out everything we could ever want for our satisfaction? Only a fool would be lured away by such a trap when all the goodness of God is available by His grace. Likewise, our flesh can be compared to a well of stagnant water. It is ludicrous to believe we could be satisfied by drinking from it when we can come to the fountain of Living Water Himself who gives us every good and perfect gift.

God's Stability

*The Father of lights, with whom
there is no variation or shadow of turning.*

James 1:17

James called God "the Father of lights," which was an ancient Jewish reference to God as the Creator. James chose that title because it fit his illustration of God.

The lights are the sun, moon, and stars—celestial bodies created by God. From our perspective, the sun, moon, and stars move, disappear, change in shape, or vary in intensity—their benefit to us comes and goes. But with God there is no variation or shifting. God doesn't change from one condition to another or shift like shadows as the sun moves. His brilliant light of glory and gracious goodness does not fade. His grace never goes dark. First John 1:5 says, "God is light and in Him is no darkness at all." Malachi 3:6 says, "I am the Lord, I do not change."

God's mercy never ceases. Nothing can eclipse His goodness or stop His benevolence. Knowing that, don't take the devil's bait and give birth to deadly sin. Rather, receive the good that God wants to give you.

Stability

November

ATTACK ON THE CHURCH

In the world you will have tribulation.

JOHN 16:33

We shouldn't be surprised when the church comes under attack because Christ said it would happen. Because the world, the flesh, and the devil are behind such hostility, Christ instructed us to "watch and pray, lest [we] enter into temptation" (Matt. 26:41). Peter warned, "Be sober, be vigilant, because your adversary the devil walks about like a roaring lion, seeking whom he may devour" (1 Pet. 5:8). To be prepared, Paul said, "Let us who are of the day be sober, putting on the breastplate of faith and love, and as a helmet the hope of salvation" (1 Thess. 5:8).

It can be difficult to maintain your Christian testimony when persecution is subtle rather than open. I remember asking a Russian pastor, "Is it difficult to pastor a church in your country?" The pastor responded, "No, it's easy because I know where everyone stands. But how can someone pastor a church in America, where compromise is so common and subtle?" Many so-called Christians want the world's acceptance and are therefore unwilling to take a stand for Christ.

STAND FIRM

Stand fast in the Lord.

PHILIPPIANS 4:1

Today's verse calls to mind a picture of a soldier standing his ground in the midst of battle. Paul used the same metaphor in Ephesians 6:11: "Put on the whole armor of God, that you may be able to stand against the wiles of the devil." Standing fast or firm spiritually means not compromising your Christian testimony in allowing yourself to be overwhelmed by trials or temptation.

It saddens me that many believers don't take God and His commands seriously enough. Instead of wanting to know God, many prefer to be entertained. That kind of apathy regards His commands as mere suggestions. But our sovereign Lord commands us to stand firm. Inherent in that command is the capacity to obey.

PAUL'S CARE
FOR THE CHURCH

*For God is my witness, how greatly I long
for you all with the affection of Jesus Christ.*

PHILIPPIANS 1:8

The apostle Paul treated believers with a gracious and tender spirit—he often tempered commands with genuine expressions of love for the people. He had a special place in his heart for the Philippian church. He addressed those believers as his "beloved and longed-for brethren" (Phil. 4:1).

He manifested his love in his desire to remain with them for their "progress and joy in the faith"(1:25). Indeed Paul was willing to be offered "on the sacrifice and service of [their] faith" (2:17). And only the Philippian believers had "shared with [him] concerning giving and receiving" (4:15), which also reveals his special bond with them.

Paul was a logician and theologian without equal—his intellectual capacity was staggering—but he was also endowed with a tremendous capacity to love people. Your ministry can be effective only when you love people.

PAUL'S JOY

My beloved and longed-for brethren,
my joy and crown.

PHILIPPIANS 4:1

The apostle Paul's joy came from fellow believers. Today's verse says the Philippian believers were his "joy and crown." To the Thessalonian believers he likewise proclaimed, "What is our hope, or joy, or crown of rejoicing? Is it not even you in the presence of our Lord Jesus Christ at His coming? For you are our glory and joy" (1 Thess. 2:19–20).

Paul rejoiced in the church's salvation and spiritual growth, which is represented by the word *crown*. The term refers to a laurel wreath, something an athlete received in biblical times for winning a contest (1 Cor. 9:25). But an athlete wasn't the only recipient of such a wreath. If someone was honored by his peers, he too would receive one as the guest of honor at a great feast or banquet. The wreath then was symbolic of success or a fruitful life. The Philippian believers were Paul's reward—proof that his efforts were successful. As you minister your gifts, may you experience the kind of joy Paul had.

A Good Soldier

*You therefore must endure
hardship as a good soldier of Jesus Christ.*

2 Timothy 2:3

Courage, conviction, and integrity are respectable qualities from a secular viewpoint, yet it is essential that they be manifested in the life of every Christian. That's because the name "Christian" identifies us with Christ, who never compromised or deviated from the truth. He is the perfect example of courageous integrity.

It stands to reason, then, that we are called to be stable and steadfast like Christ and not waver (James 1:6). Injunctions to stand firm (Eph. 6:11, 13–14) and be strong (1 Cor. 16:13; 2 Tim. 2:1) affirm that we are to be bold and uncompromising in living for Jesus Christ.

Most of us earnestly desire to stand firm and not stumble in our Christian walk. None of us wants to be crushed under the weight of life's trials or be defeated by the onslaught from the world, the flesh, and the devil. But we must realize that standing firm and being strong isn't easy because we are engaged in spiritual warfare (2 Tim. 2:3–4). We have to be prepared to "endure hardship" along the way—as a "good soldier" of faith.

DEALING WITH DISUNITY

*Stand fast in one spirit, with one mind
striving together for the faith of the gospel.*

PHILIPPIANS 1:27

Spiritual stability depends on mutual love, harmony, and peace between believers. Our lives are to be intertwined that we might support and sustain one other.

In today's verse, we read that Paul wanted that kind of harmony in the Philippian church, but instead there was an intense disagreement between two women threatening the church's life. Paul sought to keep sins such as partiality, criticism, bitterness, unforgiveness, and pride from spreading throughout the church.

To avoid such problems, it is necessary for believers to care and pray for each other. Mutual love produces the harmony that's conducive to spiritual stability and reflects what the church is all about: supporting the weak, lifting the fallen, and restoring the broken.

NOVEMBER 7

A Plea for Unity

Fulfill my joy by being likeminded,
having the same love, being of one accord, of one mind.

PHILIPPIANS 2:2

The apostle Paul was a great theologian, which meant he often addressed important doctrinal issues. He opposed the legalism of the Judaizers (Phil. 3:2) and the libertine views of other false teachers (vv. 18–19). He knew such teachings perverted the doctrine of salvation and threatened the church's life. Yet he also realized that discord in the church was an equal threat to its life. That's because conflict robs the church of its power and destroys its testimony. Enemies of Christ are eager to find ways to discredit the church.

Apparently, disunity in the Philippian church was about to destroy the integrity of its testimony. So Paul said to them, "Only let your conduct be worthy of the gospel of Christ, so that whether I come and see you or am absent, I may hear of your affairs, that you stand fast in one spirit, with one mind striving together for the faith of the gospel" (1:27). We have one Spirit within us, so there's no reason for disunity.

AVOID PERSONAL CONFLICT

*I implore Euodia and I implore
Syntyche to be of the same mind in the Lord.*

PHILIPPIANS 4:2

Paul faced many conflicts in the church, but some were important enough for him to deal with in his epistles, and thus are important enough for our instruction. Evidently the two women in today's verse were leading two opposing factions in the church. We don't know what their specific complaints were, but we can surmise it was a personal conflict.

We do know the two women were prominent church members because they had worked with Paul in the cause of the gospel (Phil. 4:3). And we know they were creating havoc in the church because it apparently was not united (Phil. 2:2). Recognizing the issue to be a lack of love—which indicates the presence of pride and the absence of humility—Paul pleaded for the women "to be of the same mind in the Lord" (4:2). Each was demanding her own way rather than being concerned about the other. But as Paul encouraged them and us, a right relationship with the Lord will resolve any discord.

Rejoice in the Lord

Rejoice in the Lord always.
Again I will say, rejoice.
Philippians 4:4

Many believers allow themselves to be victimized by their circumstances and consequently vacillate between a spiritual high and low. For them, a command to rejoice seems unreasonable. But the command of today's verse is to rejoice "in the Lord."

We can't always rejoice in our circumstances or other people because both can be bad. However, we can rejoice in the Lord because He is always good and we know He never changes. Thus, our spiritual stability directly relates to our knowledge of God. Knowing Him helps us live above our circumstances and provides stability. That's why the Psalms were written in poetic form and meter and set to music—so the people of Israel could memorize Scripture and sing hymns to deepen their knowledge of God. Knowing Him makes everything else seem less significant.

REASONS FOR REJOICING

Though now you do not see Him, yet believing,
you rejoice with joy inexpressible and full of glory.

1 PETER 1:8

Christians have many reasons for rejoicing. The primary one is based on who God is—He is sovereign. That is the single greatest truth about God. Nothing is outside His control, and He controls everything to work out ultimately for our good (Rom. 8:28). He has an infinite understanding of every aspect of our lives—where we are and what we say (Ps. 139:2–4). And He exercises His understanding in perfect wisdom. Knowing God like that should give us inexpressible and glorious joy.

We should also rejoice because God saved us, adopted us, and promised to give us an inheritance in Jesus Christ (Eph. 1:1–11). When Christ returns, we will enjoy His presence and the heavenly place prepared for us (John 14:2–3). Until then, we have joy in knowing God has promised to supply all our needs (Phil. 4:19). Furthermore, we have the privilege of serving the One we supremely love. That includes sharing the good news with the lost and encouraging fellow Christians to grow in their love and service for Him. We can also have joy in knowing we can pray to God at any time (Heb. 4:15–16).

LIKE A TREE FIRMLY PLANTED

He will be like a tree firmly planted by streams of water,
which yields its fruit in its season, and its leaf does not wither;
and in whatever he does, he prospers.

PSALM 1:3, NASB

Many people in society want to live a more stable life. To those who are filled with anxiety and unable to cope with their circumstances, the world offers a myriad of solutions that don't work.

Unfortunately, many churches have followed the world in believing that man can only solve his problems through secular psychology—a product that can't live up to its promises.

Where can you find stability? The answer is in Psalm 1. It begins, "How blessed is the man who does not walk in the counsel of the wicked, nor stand in the path of sinners!" (v. 1, NASB) and ends, "Therefore the wicked will not stand in the judgment . . . For the Lord knows the way of the righteous, but the way of the wicked will perish" (vv. 5–6).

The person who walks with God knows stability, but the one who rejects Him flounders in meaningless existence. Which would you rather be?

HUMILITY AND GRACE

Let your forbearing spirit be known to all men.

PHILIPPIANS 4:5, NASB

It is difficult to find one English word that captures the diverse meaning of the word translated as "forbearing" in today's verse. Some say it speaks of contentment, gentleness, generosity, or good-will toward others. Others believe it refers to mercy or leniency toward the faults or failures of others. Still others claim it describes patience, referring to someone who submits to injustice or mistreatment but doesn't retaliate with hatred or bitterness. I believe the best translation is "graciousness," because in the Christian sense that word embodies all the other meanings.

Forbearance also includes another important element: humility. The humble Christian doesn't hold a grudge but trusts God whenever he is mistreated, misjudged, or misrepresented. A person like that doesn't demand his rights. God manifested His grace to us in the same way—mankind abused and maligned Jesus Christ though He deserved none of it, yet He still reached out to us in love (cf. Rom. 5:10). Humility and graciousness will help you be stable in spite of the circumstances.

THE SOURCE
OF CONTENTMENT

I have learned in whatever state I am, to be content.

PHILIPPIANS 4:4

Existentialism, the dominant mindset of contemporary psychology, has infiltrated not only our country but also many churches. It implies that every man has the right to do whatever makes him feel good. But wrong thinking like that stems from self-centered pride. It's the selfish person who says, "If it makes you feel good but hurts me, you can't do it. But if it makes me feel good but hurts you, I can do it anyway." Some deceive themselves by thinking their sin doesn't hurt anyone, but sin always ends up hurting.

In contrast to self-love, Scripture says we're to be humble and unselfish (Phil. 2:3–4), love those who mistreat us (Matt. 5:44), and extend mercy toward those who stumble repeatedly (1 Pet. 4:8). Those qualities enabled Paul to be content in any circumstances. In contrast, some believers take all that they hear and see and filter it through their minds to see if it wounds them in any way, which will result in immediate instability and anxiety.

When others mistreat you, humility will help you keep your balance.

The Lord Is Near

The Lord is at hand.
Be anxious for nothing.
PHILIPPIANS 4:5–6

The Lord Jesus Christ encompasses all believers with His presence (Ps. 119:151). When you have a thought, the Lord is near to read it; when you pray, the Lord is near to hear it; when you need His strength and power, He is near to provide it. In fact, He lives in you and is the source of your spiritual life. An awareness of His presence will keep you from being anxious or unstable.

Knowing the Lord is near helps us "be anxious for nothing" because we know He can handle everything we encounter. Fretting and worrying indicate a lack of trust in God. Either you've created another god who can't help you, or else you believe God could help you but refuses, which means you are questioning His integrity and Word. So delight in the Lord and meditate on His Word (Ps. 1:2). Know who He is and how He acts. Then you'll be able to say, "The Lord is near, so I'm not going to worry."

AN ANCHOR
OF CONFIDENCE

In you, O Lord, I put my trust; let me
never be ashamed; deliver me in Your righteousness.

PSALM 31:1

As today's verse indicates, David trusted God mightily in the midst of severe hardship. He also said, "For You are my rock and my fortress; therefore, for Your name's sake, lead me and guide me. Pull me out of the net which they have secretly laid for me, for You are my strength" (Ps. 31:3–4). His trust rested in the character of God. An adequate knowledge of God is essential for spiritual stability. And the only way to know God is through what He has chosen to reveal of Himself in Scripture.

Sovereign Control

*Elect according to
the foreknowledge of God.*

1 Peter 1:2

Through the years, Arminian and Calvinistic theologies have been at opposite poles. Traditional Reformed theology, which we call Calvinism, emphasizes God's sovereignty, but Arminian theology in effect emphasizes man's sovereignty. It teaches that God is helpful in providing spiritual assistance, but that one must find it in himself to come to Christ, persevere in the faith, accomplish spiritual goals, and win spiritual victories.

What results from that kind of theology? A person can profess to trust in Christ, but in reality trusts in himself. This reflects the belief that the power to choose salvation—or lose it through spiritual failure—belongs to the individual. Suppose you believed you had that kind of power. Can you imagine what it would be like to face death and wonder if you would be disqualified from heaven because you had committed too many sins? That kind of uncertainty will bring anxiety, not security.

Fully trusting God requires an understanding of His sovereign grace: that an individual is chosen, redeemed, kept, and glorified by God, who is the initiator.

React to Problems
with Thankful Prayer

In everything by prayer
and supplication, with thanksgiving,
let your requests be made known to God.

Philippians 4 : 6

Instead of praying to God with doubt or dis-
contentment, the believer is to approach God
in a spirit of thanksgiving. That's because God
promised not to allow anything into our lives that will
be too much for us to bear (1 Cor. 10:13). He has
promised to work out everything for our good (Rom.
8:28), and "perfect, establish, strengthen, and settle" us
in the midst of our suffering (1 Pet. 5:10).

All difficulties are within God's purpose, so we can
thank Him for His available power and promises. Peter
said to cast "all your care upon Him, for He cares for
you" (1 Pet. 5:7). In doing so, we are to be thankful for
His providence, His promise of perfecting us, the glory
He will receive from accomplishing His will, and for
past mercies that are the promise of future blessings.

HEAVENLY PEACE

The peace of God,
which surpasses all understanding.

PHILIPPIANS 4:7

 Today's verse promises inner calm or tranquility to the believer who prays with a thankful attitude. Notice it doesn't promise what the answer to our prayers will be.

This peace "surpasses all understanding," which refers to its divine origin. It transcends human intellect, analysis, and insight. No human counselor can give it to you because it's a gift from God.

The real challenge of Christian living is not to eliminate every uncomfortable circumstance from your life, but to trust the infinite, holy, sovereign, and powerful God in the midst of every situation.

Jesus said, "These things I have spoken to you, that in Me you may have peace. In the world you will have tribulation; but be of good cheer, I have overcome the world" (John 16:33). So begin to live on the supernatural plane, accept that you live in a fallen world, and allow God to do His perfect work in you. And God will give you His peace as you confidently entrust yourself to His care.

THE GUARDIANSHIP OF PEACE

The peace of God . . . will guard
your hearts and minds through Christ Jesus.

PHILIPPIANS 4:7

Today's verse speaks of God's peace guarding our hearts and minds. "Will guard" is a military term meaning, "to keep watch over." The Philippian believers lived in a garrison town where Roman soldiers were stationed to guard the interests of the empire in that part of the world. In the same way, God's peace guards us from anxiety, doubt, fear, and distress.

The believer who doesn't live in the confidence of God's sovereignty will lack His peace and be left to the chaos of a troubled heart. But our confident trust in the Lord will allow us to thank Him in the midst of trials because we have God's peace on duty to protect our hearts and minds.

When Paul refers to our hearts and minds, he isn't making a distinction between the two—it's a comprehensive statement that describes the whole inner person. Because of our union with Christ, He guards our entire being with His peace. And that's what helps us be spiritually stable.

JONAH'S THANKSGIVING

I will sacrifice to you with the voice of thanksgiving;
I will pay what I have vowed. Salvation is of the Lord.

 Amazingly, the prophet Jonah gave thanks to God while he was in the great fish's belly (Jon. 2:1). How would you respond if you were Jonah? Maybe you would cry out, "What are You doing, God? Where are You? Why is this happening?" But Jonah reacted differently: "I cried out to the Lord because of my affliction, and He answered me. Out of the belly of Sheol I cried, and You heard My voice" (v. 2). He then described his sinking into the sea and the severity of his dilemma (vv. 3–5)

Nevertheless, in the midst of such great trauma, Jonah prayed, "You have brought up my life from the pit, O Lord, my God. When my soul fainted within me, I remembered the Lord; and my prayer went up to You, into Your holy temple" (vv. 6–7). Although he had his weaknesses, Jonah reflected great spiritual stability in his prayer. He was confident of God's ability to deliver him if He so chose. In the same way, the peace of God will help you if you react to circumstances with thankful prayer.

NOVEMBER 21

RIGHT THINKING

These were more noble-minded than those in Thessalonica,
in that they received the word with all readiness, and searched
the Scriptures daily to find out whether these things were so.

ACTS 17:11

It's frightening to realize our culture has more interest in emotion and pragmatism than in thinking. That's evident when people more often ask, "How will it make me feel?" instead of "Is it true?" That wrong focus is also evident in today's theology, where the predominant questions are "Will it divide?" and "Will it offend?" rather than "Is it right?" Not enough people are like the people of Berea, whom the Bible describes as being "noble-minded" because they were interested in finding truth, not good feelings or pleasant circumstances.

Too many people are going to church today not to think or reason about the truth, but to get a certain feeling. But living by emotions rather than right thinking will produce instability. In his book *Your Mind Matters*, John Stott explains this point: "Sin has more dangerous effects on our faculty of feeling than on our faculty of thinking, because our opinions are more easily checked and regulated by revealed truth than our experiences."

Too Little Thought

For "who has known the mind of the Lord that he
may instruct Him?" But we have the mind of Christ.

1 Corinthians 2:16

Some people assume worry is the result of too much thinking. But in reality it's the result of too little thinking in the right direction. When we were saved, we received a new mind or way of thinking. Now our human thought patterns are injected with divine and supernatural ones.

The apostle Paul said, "For those who live according to the flesh set their minds on the things of the flesh, but those who live according to the Spirit, the things of the Spirit. For to be carnally minded is death, but to be spiritually minded is life and peace" (Rom. 8:5–6). Because of the Spirit of God in our lives, we think on a spiritual level, not a fleshly one.

Paul also said, "Of Him you are in Christ Jesus, who became for us wisdom from God—and righteousness and sanctification and redemption" (1 Cor. 1:30). Since God imparts His wisdom to us, we can think the deep thoughts of the eternal God.

A Renewed Knowledge

Put on the new man who is renewed in
knowledge according to the image of Him who created him.

We live in a fallen world, and as a result, our renewed minds need ongoing cleansing and refreshment. God's chief agent of purifying our thinking is His Word (John 15:3; Eph. 5:26).

The New Testament calls us to the mental discipline of right thinking. Colossians 3:2 says, "Set your mind on things above, not on things on earth." First Peter 1:13 says, "Gird up the loins of your mind, be sober, and rest your hope fully upon . . . the revelation of Jesus Christ." And Paul often instructed his listeners to think right and not be ignorant.

The Old Testament also calls us to right thinking. King Solomon said, "Incline your ear to wisdom, and apply your heart to understanding; yes, if you cry for discernment, and lift up your voice for understanding, . . . then you will understand the fear of the Lord, and find the knowledge of God" (Prov. 2:2–5).

Dwelling on the right things takes initiative and effort. But if you are faithful to make the maximum effort, God will give you understanding (cf. Ps. 119:34).

MEDITATE ON THESE THINGS

*Whatever things are true, whatever things are noble,
whatever things are just, whatever things are pure,
whatever things are lovely, whatever things are of good report,
if there is any virtue and if there is anything praiseworthy
—meditate on these things.*

PHILIPPIANS 4:8

 Today's verse gives a comprehensive list of the types of things we should be dwelling on.

True things. You will find what is true in God's Word.

Noble things. We are to think about whatever is worthy of awe and adoration—the sacred as opposed to the profane.

Just things. Right thinking is always consistent with God's absolute holiness.

Pure things. This refers to something morally clean and undefiled.

Lovely things. This means "pleasing" or "amiable."

Good report. This speaks of that which is highly regarded or well thought of.

Virtue and praiseworthy things. This refers to what is reputable in the world at large, such as kindness, courtesy, and respect for others.

Content and Confident

Uphold my steps in Your paths,
that my footsteps may not slip.

Psalm 17:5

Christians who are spiritually stable have a testimony that honors Christ. That's the kind of testimony the apostle Paul had. Bound in chains as a prisoner of the Roman Empire, he remained content and confident in the Lord (Phil. 4:11, 13). Yet so many believers are not confident. In fact, unbelievers find it difficult to understand how a Christian who believes in an all-sufficient God can live as though God were weak.

Perhaps there have been times when you felt crushed, weak, and unable to stand. You know what it's like to lose your spiritual balance. We face strong temptations and trials in this life. Nevertheless, it's vital for us to be spiritually stable not only for our own well being but also for our Christian testimony before the lost world. So make sure you are depending on God to help you stand, not on yourself.

ARRESTING THE FLESH

How can a young man cleanse his way?
By taking heed according to your word.

PSALM 119:8

The godly conduct that produces spiritual stability depends on obeying the divine standard of God's Word. The Word is what cultivates godly attitudes, thoughts, and actions that will keep you from being overwhelmed by trials and temptations.

To understand the relationship between godly attitudes, thoughts, and actions, consider this analogy. If a policeman sees someone who is about to violate the law, he will arrest him. Similarly, godly attitudes and thoughts produced by the Word act as policemen to arrest the flesh before it commits a crime against the standard of God's Word. But if they are not on duty, they can't arrest the flesh, and the flesh is free to violate the law of God.

The analogy teaches that right attitudes and thoughts must precede right practices. Paul realized only spiritual weapons will help in our warfare against the flesh (2 Cor. 10:4). By using the right weapons, you can take "every thought into captivity to the obedience of Christ" (v. 5).

LOSE THOSE BAD HABITS

The work of righteousness will be peace,
and the effect of righteousness,
quietness and assurance forever.

ISAIAH 32:17

Pure behavior produces spiritual peace and stability, but sinful behavior produces instability. That is true not only in the millennial kingdom, where Christ one day will rule the earth in righteousness, as today's verse indicates, but also in the life of the believer. James the brother of Jesus said, "The wisdom that is from above is first pure, then peaceable. . . . Now the fruit of righteousness is sown in peace by those who make peace" (James 3:17–18).

Contentment, comfort, calm, quietness, and tranquility accompany godly conduct, which is based on God's Word. Doing good is not only the way to overcome evil (Rom. 12:21), but also the expected practice of every believer. As you cultivate godly habits by the power of God, your bad habits will diminish, and your life will become more stable.

THE PROPHETIC WORD

We have the prophetic word confirmed,
which you do well to heed as a light that shines
in a dark place, until the day dawns and the
morning star arises in your hearts.

2 PETER 1:19

The Philippian believers had the Old Testament books to go to, but the entire New Testament had yet to be completed at the time Paul wrote his letter to them. Since they may have had access to only a minimal amount of written revelation in the New Testament, the believers looked to the apostles as their source of truth until all the New Testament books were brought together. So the standard of Christian belief and behavior was embodied in the teaching and example of the apostles.

That's why on the day of Pentecost three thousand believers "continued steadfastly in the apostles' doctrine" (Acts 2:42). That's also why Paul said to the Corinthian believers, "Imitate me, just as I also imitate Christ" (1 Cor. 11:1). But you have an advantage they didn't—you have God's complete revelation available to you. So don't fail to use it.

Practice Makes Perfect

*The things you learned and received
and heard and saw in me, these things do.*

PHILIPPIANS 4:9

In today's verse, the apostle Paul emphasizes that the Philippian believers needed to practice what they learned, received, heard, and saw in his life.

First, they *learned* from his personal instruction, which included preaching, teaching, and discipling (cf. Acts 20:20). He expounded Old Testament truths and the meaning of New Testament revelation, explaining how it applied to their lives.

Next, what they received from Paul was the direct revelation from God. Scripture makes it clear that Paul received direct revelation from the Lord and then made it known to the believers (cf. 1 Cor. 11:2; 15:1–3; 1 Thess. 4:1).

From other sources, they also *heard* about Paul's character, lifestyle, and preaching. They were aware of his impeccable reputation.

And what the Philippian believers *saw* in Paul they knew to be true from firsthand experience.

Like Paul, your life should be worthy of imitation by other believers. So "be doers of the word, and not hearers only, deceiving yourselves" (James 1:22).

THE GOD OF PEACE

The God of peace will be with you.

PHILIPPIANS 4:9

The apostle Paul often referred to the Lord as the God of peace. In Romans he said, "Now the God of peace be with you all" (15:33). In 2 Corinthians he wrote, "The God of love and peace will be with you" (13:11). And to the Thessalonian believers he said, "Now may the Lord of peace Himself give you peace always in every way" (2 Thess. 3:16).

Today's verse emphasizes the fact that God's character is peace. He is the origin and giver of peace. When we have godly attitudes, thoughts, and actions, the peace of God and the God of peace will guard us. His peace provides comfort, tranquility, quietness, and confidence in the midst of any trial you may face.

Christ

DECEMBER

DECEMBER 1

The Measure
of Spiritual Maturity

In this I rejoice, yes; and will rejoice.

PHILIPPIANS 1:18

A believer's spiritual maturity can be measured by what it takes to steal his joy. Joy is a fruit of a Spirit-controlled life (Gal. 5:22). We are to rejoice always (Phil. 4:4; 1 Thess. 5:16). In all circumstances the Holy Spirit produces joy, so there ought not to be any time when we are not rejoicing in some way.

Change, confusion, trials, attacks, unmet desires, conflict, and strained relationships can throw us off balance and rob us of our joy if we're not careful. It's then we should cry out like the psalmist, "Restore to me the joy of Your salvation" (Ps. 51:12).

Jesus said, "In the world you will have tribulation" (John 16:33), and the apostle James said, "Count it all joy when you fall into various trials" (James 1:2). God has His own profound purpose in our afflictions, but He never takes away our joy. To maintain our joy we must adopt God's perspective regarding our trials. When we yield to the working of His Spirit in our lives, our difficulties will not overwhelm us.

THE REJOICING APOSTLE

My brethren, rejoice in the Lord.

PHILIPPIANS 3:1

The apostle Paul's joy was unrelated to his circumstances. If it had been tied to pleasures on earth, possessions, freedom, prestige, outward success, or a good reputation, he wouldn't have had any joy.

Paul's joy was centered on his ministry and was indifferent toward all other things. That's why he could tell the Philippians, "I thank my God upon every remembrance of you, always in every prayer of mine making request for you with all joy" (Phil. 1:3–4). He had joy in spite of trouble, as long as Christ's cause was advanced. He had joy in spite of detractors, as long as Christ's name was proclaimed. He had joy in spite of death, as long as Christ was exalted. And he had joy in spite of the flesh, as long as Christ's church was assisted.

WHAT MAKES YOU TICK?

I became a minister according to the
stewardship from God which was given to me for you.

COLOSSIANS 1:25

What motivates you? What takes all your energy, dominates your time, and makes you tick? For the apostle Paul, it was the progress of the gospel. What might happen to his own body or career was of little consequence to him. In Acts 20:24 he said, "Nor do I count my life dear to myself, so that I may finish my race with joy, and the ministry which I received from the Lord Jesus." He yielded up his life, possessions, clothes, recognition, reputation, and prestige to one goal: "to testify solemnly of the gospel of the grace of God" (v. 24).

To the church in Rome Paul wrote, "I am ready to preach the gospel to you who are in Rome also" (Rom. 1:15). And in 1 Corinthians 9:16 he testifies to what compelled him, "Necessity is laid upon me; yes, woe is me if I do not preach the gospel."

Paul was driven to see the gospel move forward—he is a model for every Christian. Is your life like Paul's?

A Prisoner for Christ

It has become evident to the whole palace guard,
and to all the rest, that my chains are in Christ.

PHILIPPIANS 1:13

 The apostle Paul always saw himself as a prisoner because of Christ—never because of crime. He was in chains because he believed in, preached, and represented Jesus Christ.

From the point of view of Rome, Paul was a captive chained to a Roman guard. But from Paul's perspective, the Roman guards were captives chained to him! The result of such close confinement was that the cause of Christ had "become evident to the whole palace guard." Far from being a burdensome condition, Paul had been given the opportunity to witness for Christ to each guard assigned to him, at six hours a stretch.

What did those soldiers see? They saw Paul's godly character, graciousness, patience, love, wisdom, and conviction. As members of the palace guard were converted, salvation spread beyond them to "those who are of Caesar's household" (Phil. 4:22). No matter how difficult it may appear on the surface, no one is too difficult to reach with the gospel.

SEEING THE REALITY
OF A TRANSFORMED LIFE

Paul dwelt two whole years in his own rented house,
and received all who came to him, preaching the kingdom of
God and teaching the things which concern the Lord Jesus Christ
with all confidence, no one forbidding him.

ACTS 28:30–31

Today's verse shows that while Paul was under house arrest "in his own rented house," he continued to minister. In spite of the circumstances, Paul continued to do what he had been called to do.

You may find yourself thinking, *I can't go and preach the gospel. I can't be an evangelist, or a Bible teacher. I'm stuck with my job.* But it doesn't matter whether you're chained to a desk, an assembly line, a classroom, a car, or a sales position—they all provide opportunities for you to further the gospel. The worse your confinement, the greater the opportunity for a godly life to shine.

People often tell me how hard it is to witness where they work. My response is that it is generally harder to witness under ideal conditions than in a more difficult situation. That's because in difficult situations the reality of a transformed life is more apparent, and that can't help but be attractive to those who haven't experienced it.

GAINING COURAGE

Most of the brethren in the Lord,
having become confident by my chains,
are much more bold to speak the word without fear.

PHILIPPIANS 1:14

The implication of today's verse is that before Paul's imprisonment, the church in Rome lacked courage. When the believers saw that God provided for Paul and enabled him to have an incredible opportunity for outreach, they confidently began to proclaim the gospel. They realized that since God could minister through Paul in his condition, He could minister through them as well. As Paul's strength became theirs, the leadership in Rome began "to speak the word without fear" (v. 14).

Does your joy ebb and flow according to the tide of earthly benefits? Do pleasure, possessions, prominence, prestige, reputation, comfort, and fulfillment or your own ambitions propel your joy? If they do, your joy will ebb and flow according to the shifting tides of life. But if your joy is tied to the progress of the gospel, it will never diminish. Fix your heart on the progress of the gospel, and your joy will be constant.

DISTRESS IN THE MINISTRY

Some indeed preach Christ . . . from selfish ambition,
not sincerely, supposing to add affliction to my chains.

PHILIPPIANS 1:15–16

I am often asked, "What has been the most discouraging thing in your ministry?" As far as I can remember, my answer has remained consistent over the years.

There are two issues that deeply distress me. One is seeing those who ought to be the most mature in the faith—the ones who know the Word of God well, have experienced the blessings of spiritual growth and fellowship, and have seen God's power demonstrated time and again—turn their backs on the faith and embrace sin. That's much more discouraging than when a new, untrained Christian falls into sin through ignorance.

The second is being falsely accused by fellow preachers of the gospel. Some men seem to desire to discredit the ministry of others. As a result, they falsely accuse other ministers, not because they have valid reasons, but simply for the satisfaction of discrediting them.

As you live a godly life, expect that your service to God will be attacked. But don't let that affect your joy.

THE BLESSING OF SUPPORTERS

*Some indeed preach Christ even from
envy and strife, and some also from goodwill.*

PHILIPPIANS 1:15

It hurts to think of so dear a saint as Paul enduring opposition to the point of reporting, "At my first defense [the first trial in Rome] no one stood with me, but all forsook me" (2 Tim. 4:16). When Paul wrote to the Philippians, he was so bereft of friends that he said of Timothy, "I have no one like-minded" (Phil. 2:20).

But Paul also wrote that some were preaching Christ "from goodwill" according to today's verse, which denotes satisfaction and contentedness. Paul's supporters were content with what God was doing in their own lives and in Paul's life. They were sympathetic toward him and grateful for his ministry.

There are also people like that today—what a blessing, encouragement, and source of joy they are! I thank God for filling my life with people like that.

What Matters Most

Only that in every way, whether in pretense or in truth,
Christ is preached; and in this I rejoice, yes, and will rejoice.

PHILIPPIANS 1:18

The word "preached" in today's verse means "to proclaim with authority." Regardless of the personal cost, Paul was determined that Christ be proclaimed with authority.

Even when Paul's detractors preached the true gospel, it had an impact. A selfishly motivated preacher can still be used of God because the truth is more powerful than the package it comes in.

Paul lived to see the gospel proclaimed—he didn't care who received the credit. That's to be the attitude of every pastor, teacher, elder, deacon, leader, and layperson in the church. In all that he suffered, Paul didn't quit, lash out, break down, or lose his joy. That's because the cause of Christ was being furthered and His name proclaimed. It was all Paul cared about. That's an attitude the grace of Christ instills in all who would be godly.

A SERVANT'S ATTITUDE

*Whoever of you does not forsake
all that he has cannot be My disciple.*

LUKE 14:33

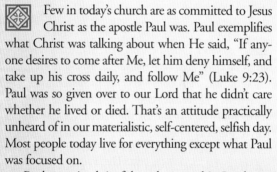 Few in today's church are as committed to Jesus Christ as the apostle Paul was. Paul exemplifies what Christ was talking about when He said, "If anyone desires to come after Me, let him deny himself, and take up his cross daily, and follow Me" (Luke 9:23). Paul was so given over to our Lord that he didn't care whether he lived or died. That's an attitude practically unheard of in our materialistic, self-centered, selfish day. Most people today live for everything except what Paul was focused on.

Paul remained joyful as long as his Lord was glorified, even when he was threatened with death. All that mattered to him was that the gospel was advanced, Christ was preached, and the Lord was magnified. The source of his joy was entirely related to the kingdom of God.

DECEMBER 11

DELIVERANCE FROM
TEMPORARY DISTRESS

I know this will turn out for my deliverance
through your prayer and the supply of the Spirit of Jesus Christ.

PHILIPPIANS 1:19

Today's verse shows the value of confident trust
in God. Paul knew his current distress was only
temporary and that he would be delivered from it.

Why was Paul convinced of his deliverance? His
statement, "I know this will turn out for my
deliverance" is a quote of the Greek version of Job
13:16. Job was a righteous man who suffered greatly,
yet he was delivered because God always delivers the
righteous. Job said, "After my skin is destroyed, this I
know, that in my flesh I shall see God" (Job 19:26). He
knew that either temporally or eternally God would
deliver him.

Paul knew he could trust God to deliver him just
as God had delivered Job. He was confident his
circumstances would work out for good, whether he
was released from prison, vindicated at his trial, and
delivered from execution or passed into glory as a
martyr. You may not face the same trials as Paul, but
whatever your circumstances, the same confident trust
is available to you.

EFFECTIVE PRAYERS

*I beg you, brethren, through the Lord Jesus Christ,
and through the love of the Spirit, that you strive
together with me in prayers to God for me.*

ROMANS 15:30

Paul was confident he would be delivered through the prayers of the saints, no matter what trial he was enduring. He believed in the sovereign will and purpose of God, and knew that He would bring His purposes to pass in concert with the prayers of His children. He also knew that "the effective, fervent prayer of a righteous man avails much" (James 5:16). Just as the love and prayers of the saints in the first century encouraged Paul greatly, your prayers on behalf of your spiritual leaders will encourage them.

SUSTENANCE
FOR THE RIGHTEOUS

Not by might nor by power, but by My Spirit.

ZECHARIAH 4:6

God's Word, prayer, and the Holy Spirit all work together for the benefit of God's servants. The Spirit's special part is to grant all that is necessary to sustain the righteous.

The Holy Spirit is called "the Spirit of Christ" and "the Spirit of God" (Rom. 8:9). He can be called by either title because He is within the Trinity and proceeds from the Father in the name of Christ (cf. John 14:26).

The apostle Paul knew the Holy Spirit as his indwelling teacher, interceder, guide, source of power, and all-sufficient provider. That's what the Spirit is for all believers. Paul's confidence in knowing that all things work together for good (Rom. 8:28) was based on the provision of the Spirit, who "helps in our weaknesses. For we do not know what we should pray for as we ought, but the Spirit Himself makes intercession for us with groanings which cannot be uttered" (v. 26).

Knowing what the Spirit provides will help you face with tremendous confidence anything that comes your way.

UNASHAMED

According to my earnest expectation and hope [I know]
that in nothing I shall be ashamed, but with all boldness,
as always, so now also Christ will be magnified in my body.

PHILIPPIANS 1:20

Today's verse calls to mind Christ's promise in Matthew 10:32: "Whoever confesses Me before men, him I will also confess before My Father who is in heaven." The one who acknowledges Christ as Lord in life or in death, if necessary, is the one whom the Lord will acknowledge before God as His own.

The apostle Paul could rejoice in that truth. He knew he never would be ashamed before the world, the court of Caesar, or God Himself because he knew God would be glorified in his life. The Old Testament affirms that the righteous will never be put to shame, while the unrighteous will.

To be ashamed means to be disappointed, disillusioned, or disgraced. Paul knew that would never happen to him because of God's promise to the righteous. He may have had Isaiah 49:23 in mind: "They shall not be ashamed who wait for Me." Be one of the unashamed.

GOD WITH US

For there will be a fulfillment of
those things which were told her from the Lord.

LUKE 1:45

Isaiah 7:14 says, "The Lord Himself will give you a sign: Behold, a virgin will be with child and bear a son, and she will call His name Immanuel." That virgin's name was Mary.

The name *Immanuel*, however, is the key to this verse—and the heart of the Christmas story. It is a Hebrew name that means literally, "God with us." It is a promise of incarnate deity, a prophecy that God Himself would appear as a human infant, Immanuel, "God with us." This baby who was to be born would be God Himself in human form.

If we could condense all the truths of Christmas into only three words, these would be the words: "God with us." We tend to focus our attention at Christmas on the *infancy* of Christ. The greater truth of the holiday is His *deity*. More astonishing than a baby in the manger is the truth that this promised baby is the omnipotent Creator of the heavens and the earth!

PEACE ON EARTH?

Glory to God in the highest, and on earth
peace among men with whom He is pleased.

LUKE 2:14, NASB

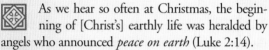 As we hear so often at Christmas, the begin-
ning of [Christ's] earthly life was heralded by
angels who announced *peace on earth* (Luke 2:14).

There never really has been peace on earth, in the
sense we think of it. Wars and rumors of wars have
characterized the entire two millennia since that first
Christmas, and all the time before it.

That announcement of peace on earth was a two-
pronged proclamation. First, it declared the arrival of
the only One who ultimately can bring lasting peace
on earth (which He will do when He returns to bring
about the final establishment of His earthly kingdom).

But more important, it was a proclamation that
God's peace is available to men and women. Read the
words of Luke 2:14 carefully: "'Glory to God in the
highest, and on earth peace among men *with whom He
is pleased.*'"

Who are those with whom He is pleased? The ones
who have yielded their lives to the authority of His
government.

Christians and Christmas

He who observes the day, observes it to the Lord.

The Puritans in early America rejected Christmas celebrations altogether. They deliberately worked on December 25 to show their disdain. A law passed in England in 1644 reflected a similar Puritan influence; the law made Christmas Day an official working day. For a time in England it was literally illegal to cook plum pudding or mince pie for the holidays.

Christians today are generally not opposed to celebrating Christmas. The holiday itself is nothing, and observing it is not a question of right or wrong. As Paul wrote, "One man regards one day above another, another regards every day alike. Let each man be fully convinced in his own mind. He who observes the day, observes it for the Lord, and he who eats, does so for the Lord, for he gives thanks to God; and he who eats not, for the Lord he does not eat, and gives thanks to God" (Rom. 14:5–6). Every day—including Christmas—is a celebration for us who know and love Him.

CHRIST'S GRACE TO SINNERS

For I did not come to call the righteous,
but sinners, to repentance.

MATTHEW 9:13

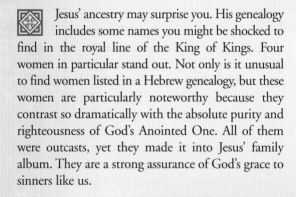 Jesus' ancestry may surprise you. His genealogy includes some names you might be shocked to find in the royal line of the King of Kings. Four women in particular stand out. Not only is it unusual to find women listed in a Hebrew genealogy, but these women are particularly noteworthy because they contrast so dramatically with the absolute purity and righteousness of God's Anointed One. All of them were outcasts, yet they made it into Jesus' family album. They are a strong assurance of God's grace to sinners like us.

A Message of Grace

You shall call His name JESUS.
For He will save His people from their sins.

MATTHEW 1:21

You may skip the genealogy when you read the Christmas story aloud. But don't overlook its message of grace, which after all is the heart of the Christmas story: God in His mercy doing for sinners what they cannot do for themselves—mending broken lives and restoring shattered hopes. That's why He came—to save His people from their sins (Matt. 1:21).

Here's the best part: the same grace that was evident in the genealogy is active today, and the same Jesus is saving His people from their sins. No sin, no matter how heinous, puts sinners beyond His reach. "He is able to save them to the uttermost that come unto God by him, seeing he ever liveth to make intercession for them" (Heb. 7:25, KJV).

THE CHRISTMAS TREE

The glory of Lebanon will come to you.

ISAIAH 60:13

  Christmas trees seem to have their origins in the ancient celebrations of Saturnalia. The Romans decorated their temples with greenery and candles. Roman soldiers conquering the British Isles found Druids who worshiped mistletoe and Saxons who used holly and ivy in religious ceremonies. All those things found their way into Christmas customs.

Interestingly, however, the first person to have lighted a Christmas tree may have been Martin Luther, father of the Reformation. He introduced the practice of putting candles on trees to celebrate Christmas, citing Isaiah 60:13 as biblical authority for the practice: "The glory of Lebanon will come to you, the juniper, the box tree, and the cypress together, to beautify the place of My sanctuary; and I shall make the place of My feet glorious."

CHRIST'S VIRGIN BIRTH

After His mother Mary was betrothed
to Joseph, before they came together, she was
found with child of the Holy Spirit.

MATTHEW 1:18

The virgin birth is an underlying assumption in *everything* the Bible says about Jesus. To throw out the virgin birth is to reject Christ's deity, the accuracy and authority of Scripture, and a host of other related doctrines that are the heart of the Christian faith. No issue is *more* important than the virgin birth to our understanding of who Jesus is. If we deny that Jesus is God, we have denied the very essence of Christianity. Everything else the Bible teaches about Christ hinges on the truth we celebrate at Christmas— that Jesus is God in human flesh. If the story of His birth is merely a fabricated or trumped-up legend, then so is the rest of what Scripture tells us about Him. The virgin birth is as crucial as the resurrection in substantiating His deity. It is not an optional truth. Anyone who rejects Christ's deity rejects Christ absolutely— even if he pretends otherwise (see 1 John 4:1–3).

NO OTHER NAME

There is no other name under heaven.

ACTS 4:12

 The angel that appeared to Joseph emphasized the meaning of Jesus' name: "She will bear a Son; and you shall call His name Jesus, for it is He who will save His people from their sins" (Matt.1:21). *Jesus*, from the Hebrew *Joshua*, or *Jehoshua*, means "Jehovah will save." The name itself was a testimony to God's salvation. But, the angel told Joseph, Mary's Son would be the very embodiment of Jehovah's salvation. He Himself would save His people from their sins.

After Jesus' resurrection, Peter, speaking before the Sanhedrin, also emphasized the importance of Jesus' name: "There is salvation in no one else; for there is no other name under heaven that has been given among men, by which we must be saved" (Acts 4:12).

NO ROOM FOR JESUS

And she brought forth her firstborn Son,
and wrapped Him in swaddling cloths, and laid Him in
a manger, because there was no room for them in the inn.

LUKE 2:7

I'm convinced that most people miss Christmas. They observe the season because culture says it's the thing to do, but the masses are utterly oblivious to the reality of what they are celebrating. So much fantasy and myth have been imposed on the holiday that people are numb to the real miracle of Christ's birth. The legitimate emotion of the holiday has given way to a maudlin and insincere self-indulgence. A newspaper I saw recently had a two-page spread featuring some man-on-the-street interviews where people offered their opinions of the real meaning of Christmas. . . . Some were sentimental, saying Christmas is a family time, a time for children, and so on. Others were humanistic, seeing Christmas as a time to celebrate love for one's fellow man, the spirit of giving, and that sort of thing. Others were crassly hedonistic, viewing Christmas as just another excuse to party. Not one person made mention of the incomprehensible miracle of God's birth as a human baby.

CHRIST'S PERFECT TIMING

When the fullness of the time had come,
God sent forth His Son.

GALATIANS 4:4

The first Christmas was perfectly timed. Galatians 4:4–5 says, "When the fullness of the time came, God sent forth His Son, born of a woman, born under the Law, in order that He might redeem those who were under the Law." What was "the fullness of the time"? God's sovereign timing. He ordered world events so everything was ready for Christ's coming and the subsequent outreach of the apostles.

Looking back at the early church, we are amazed at how quickly the gospel spread in less than a century. The sovereign hand of God is clearly evident. Christ's advent could not have been timed more propitiously.

WHY WAS JESUS BORN?

For even the Son of Man did not come to be served,
but to serve, and to give His life a ransom for many.

MARK 10:45

Here's a side to the Christmas story that isn't often told: those soft little hands, fashioned by the Holy Spirit in Mary's womb, were made so that nails might be driven through them. Those baby feet, pink and unable to walk, would one day walk up a dusty hill to be nailed to a cross. That sweet infant's head with sparkling eyes and eager mouth was formed so that someday men might force a crown of thorns onto it. That tender body, warm and soft, wrapped in swaddling clothes, would one day be ripped open by a spear.

Jesus was born to die.

Don't think I'm trying to put a damper on your Christmas spirit. Far from it—for Jesus' death, though devised and carried out by men with evil intentions, was in no sense a tragedy. In fact, it represents the greatest victory over evil anyone has ever accomplished.

LIFE OR DEATH

Whether by life or by death.

PHILIPPIANS 1:20

The apostle Paul didn't know the details of God's plan for his life, but he was confident in it, whether it meant life or death. Later he said, "I am hard-pressed between the two, having a desire to depart and be with Christ, which is far better. Nevertheless to remain in the flesh is more needful for you" (vv. 23–24). Paul preferred the joy of being in Christ's presence in heaven, but apparently he thought the Lord would let him live because he knew the Philippians needed him.

Paul rejoiced because he knew that by either his life or death Christ would be exalted. If he lived, he would be free to preach and build the church. If he died, he would be executed for Christ's sake, and his unwavering faith would serve as a trophy of Christ's grace. For Paul the issue was not his troubles, detractors, or even the possibility of his death, but whether the gospel was advancing and the Lord was being magnified.

Like Paul, you don't know the specifics of God's plan for your life. But one thing you can be sure of: in life or death you can glorify Christ.

THE BEST USE OF LIFE

For to me, to live is Christ, and to die is gain.

PHILIPPIANS 1:21

 Personalize today's verse by filling in the blanks: "For to me, to live is _____, and to die is _____." If you put *wealth* in the first blank, dying brings not gain but loss. The same is true if you selected *prestige, fame, power,* or *possessions* because none of those things remains after death: prestige is lost, fame is forgotten, power is useless, and possessions are taken by others. For today's verse to make sense as Paul wrote it, only *Christ* can fill the first blank. Otherwise, death is inevitably a loss.

Some who read this will say they put Christ in the blank. But if they think about it carefully, they will realize that what they really meant was Christ plus wealth, Christ plus power, or Christ plus possessions. Christ can't share the first blank with anything else. Those who truly live for Christ have no fear of death and make the best use of life—in both they glorify Christ.

FRUITFUL LABOR

If I live on in the flesh,
this will mean fruit from my labor.

PHILIPPIANS 1:22

The apostle Paul considered that being alive in the physical world is synonymous with fruitful labor for Christ. His use of "labor" refers to his spiritual work for the Lord, which yields spiritual fruit. Spiritual fruit may be seen in people, deeds, and words—whatever is of eternal value. That kind of fruit comes from good hard work, which is the natural activity of the godly on earth.

Paul had a strong desire to bear fruit. He wanted the Philippians to be confident in Christ and strengthened for evangelism (Phil. 1:26–27). He is reminiscent of the psalmist who said, "O God, You have taught me from my youth; and to this day I declare Your wondrous works. Now also when I am old and grayheaded, O God, do not forsake me, until I declare Your strength to this generation, Your power to everyone who is to come" (Ps. 71:17–18). That elderly man wanted to live long enough to declare God's strength and power to the next generation. May God grant you that same privilege.

CHOOSING BETWEEN
HEAVEN AND EARTH

What I shall choose I cannot tell.
For I am hard-pressed between the two.

PHILIPPIANS 1:23

Every Christian ought to feel the strain of desiring to be with Christ, yet also longing to build His church. If the Lord said to me, "You have five minutes to choose between being in heaven or on earth," I would have a difficult time making that decision. And I would want to be sure I was choosing for the right reasons. I'd have to ask myself, can I glorify Christ more in heaven or on earth?

Paul found it an impossible choice. Nevertheless, most people would choose to stay on earth. When asked why they would, most would give some selfish reason, such as, "We're getting a new house," or "I don't want to leave my kids." For Paul, nothing really mattered except glorifying Christ. When faced with the most basic of life's issues—whether it would be better to live or die—his response was, "I would be thrilled to glorify Christ in heaven or on earth. Given the choice, I can't choose." Because glorifying Christ was Paul's motivation, *where* he glorified Christ was not the issue. That ought to be true for you as well.

ABSENT FROM THE BODY, PRESENT WITH THE LORD

We are confident, yes, well pleased rather to be
absent from the body and to be present with the Lord.

2 CORINTHIANS 5:8

When a believer leaves this world, he goes immediately to be in the presence of Christ. There is no "soul sleep" or intermediate waiting place, nor does the Bible teach that there is any place called purgatory. Notice the apostle Paul's desire was "to depart and *be with Christ*" (Phil. 1:23, emphasis added).

Today's verse indicates that when we are absent from the body, which sleeps until the resurrection, our spirits are present with the Lord. Paul also told the Thessalonians that Christ "died for us, that whether we wake or sleep, we should live together with Him" (1 Thess. 5:10). Paul's point is that whether we are physically awake (alive) or physically asleep (dead), as believers we are with Christ. We are in His presence in a spiritual sense now and in a literal sense when our bodies are dead.

You can rejoice in the fact that there is no time in your life as a believer when you will ever be out of the conscious presence of Jesus Christ.

DESIRES BALANCED BY NEEDS

Nevertheless to remain in the flesh is more needful for you.
And being confident of this, I know that I shall remain and
continue with you all for your progress and joy of faith.

PHILIPPIANS 1:24–25

One mark of a spiritual man is that his own desires are balanced by the needs of others. That's the kind of man who could write, "Do nothing from selfishness or empty conceit, but with humility of mind let each of you regard one another as more important than himself; do not merely look out for your own personal interests, but also for the interests of others" (Phil 2:3–4, NASB).

The Philippian church needed Paul, as did many other churches. Paul knew they needed him badly enough that their need was likely to determine his future, which he expressed in today's verse.

Although Paul desired to be with Christ in heaven, he also wanted to remain on earth to help strengthen the church. He knew that if he stayed the church would better glorify Christ, and glorifying Christ was all he desired.

As you contemplate a new year, what is Christ asking you to commit your life to? I hope it's a desire to meet the needs of others with a humble heart.

Acknowledgments

Grateful acknowledgement is made to the following:

January 6. Ralph Waldo Emerson. *The Collected Works of Ralph Waldo Emerson*, vol. 1. Cambridge, Mass.: Harvard, 1971, p. 80.

January 16. Donald Grey Barnhouse. *Expositions of Bible Doctrines Taking the Epistle to the Romans as a Point of Departure*, vol. 1. Grand Rapids: Eerdmans, 1952, p. 72.

March 8. S. D. Gordon. *Quiet Talks with World Winners*. N.Y.: Eaton & Mains, 1908.

July 2. Richard Shelley Taylor. *The Disciplined Life*. Kansas City, Mo.: Beacon Hill, 1962, p. 22.

September 13. Thomas Watson. *A Divine Cordial*. Grand Rapids: Baker, 1981, p. 20.

November 21. John Stott. *Your Mind Matters*. Downers Grove, Ill.: InterVarsity, 1973, p. 16.

December 15–25. Taken from *The Miracle of Christmas* by John F. MacArthur Jr. Copyright © 1989 by John F. MacArthur Jr. Used by permission of Zondervan.

NOTES